Neutrality and Vulnerable States

T0373698

This book offers a timely and concise academic and historical background to the concept and practice of neutrality, a relatively new phenomenon in foreign and security policy.

It approaches two key questions: under what circumstances can permanent neutrality be applied, and what are the main ingredients of success and the causes of failure in applying permanent neutrality? By evaluating, comparing, and contrasting the two successful European case studies of Austria and Switzerland and the two challenging Asian case studies of Afghanistan and Laos, the author creates a new framework of analysis to explore the feasibility of reframing, adopting, and applying a policy of neutrality and jump start debates on the feasibility of the idea of "new neutrality". He opens the debate by asking whether, as neutrality successfully functioned as a conflict resolution tool during the Cold War, a reframed and adopted version of neutrality could also serve the needs of the twenty-first-century world order.

This is an insightful book for all scholars, students, and policymakers working in international relations, security studies, the history of neutrality, and Afghanistan studies.

Nasir A. Andisha is a diplomat and academic. His research interests include international relations, regional security, politics, and governance in South and Central Asia. He received a doctoral degree in diplomatic studies from the Australian National University in 2015. Andisha was a Fulbright fellow at the Bush School of Government in Texas A&M University (2007–2009), a fellow at the Marshall Centre for European Studies in Garmisch, Germany and the Asia Pacific Centre for Security Studies in Hawaii, USA, and attended the Executive Education Program for Leaders from South Asia at the Kennedy School of Government at Harvard University in 2012. He worked with the International Committee of Red Cross (ICRC) as a field officer (1998–2001) and taught international relations at the Institute of Diplomacy of the Ministry of Foreign Affairs of Afghanistan and Al-Beroni University in Kapisa Province, Afghanistan.

Neutrality and Vulnerable States

An Analysis of Afghanistan's Permanent Neutrality

Nasir A. Andisha

Routledge
Taylor & Francis Group

LONDON AND NEW YORK

First published 2021
by Routledge
2 Park Square, Milton Park, Abingdon, Oxon OX14 4RN

and by Routledge
52 Vanderbilt Avenue, New York, NY 10017

Routledge is an imprint of the Taylor & Francis Group, an informa business

© 2021 Nasir A. Andisha

British Library Cataloguing-in-Publication Data
A catalogue record for this book is available from the British Library

Library of Congress Cataloging-in-Publication Data
Names: Andisha, Nasir A., author.
Title: Neutrality and vulnerable states: an analysis of Afghanistan's permanent neutrality/Nasir A. Andisha.
Description: Abingdon, Oxon; New York, NY: Routledge, 2021. | Includes bibliographical references and index.
Identifiers: LCCN 2020019966 (print) | LCCN 2020019967 (ebook) | ISBN 9781138625785 (hardback) | ISBN 9780429459689 (ebook)
Subjects: LCSH: Neutrality. | Nonalignment. | Neutrality–Afghanistan. | Nonalignment–Afghanistan. | Afghanistan–Foreign relations.
Classification: LCC JZ6422 .A64 2021 (print) | LCC JZ6422 (ebook) | DDC 327.581–dc23
LC record available at https://lccn.loc.gov/2020019966
LC ebook record available at https://lccn.loc.gov/2020019967

ISBN: 978-1-138-62578-5 (hbk)
ISBN: 978-0-429-45968-9 (ebk)

Typeset in Times New Roman
by Deanta Global Publishing Services, Chennai, India

Contents

Tables

Preface

As a concept, neutrality—the choice not to participate in others' wars—has featured in interstate discourse at least since the Peloponnesian War toward the end of the fifth century BC. However, as an internationally sanctioned policy option, it was formalised during the Congress of Vienna in 1815. Ever since its popularisation as an alternative to recurring conflict facing strategically located small and vulnerable states, this apparently desirable foreign policy choice and convenient diplomatic tool for managing conflict and maintaining a balance of power has frequently been recommended, though intermittently applied. Even a cursory look at the application of permanent neutrality, that is, a formalised type of neutrality, as a state policy of well-known neutrals such as Switzerland, Sweden, Belgium, Austria, Laos, and others indicates a mixed success record.

On the other hand, unlike the concepts of war and peace, the study of neutrality has not been a theme of major academic interest in the discipline of international relations. The scant literature that does exist on the subject mainly focuses on the legal aspects of neutrality.

This book embarks on a dual challenge of explaining a complex and intertwined phenomenon of state neutrality in simplest possible terms and investigating the case of Afghanistan, a former buffer state which observed some form of neutrality in the past. It is argued that over the past two hundred years, Afghanistan has enjoyed stability and tranquillity when the country observed some form of neutrality, and therefore, a return to neutrality could be a return to normalcy and stability. To offer a structured yet simple analysis of state neutrality, this study outlines the circumstances under which permanent neutrality can be applied and illustrates the main ingredients of success and the causes of failure. The analysis of Afghanistan's history of neutrality and feasibility and desirability of neutrality as a future course is conducted with the help of a multi-factorial analytical framework drawn from the current literature and augmented through examining Swiss, Austrian, and Laotian neutrality as case studies.

The empirical examination indicates that external factors such as appropriate geo-political positions and importance, balance of power and military stalemates, consensus and agreement of the neighbouring countries and the great powers, and internal factors such as domestic stability and cohesion and military and economic capabilities of the neutral state in varying degrees contribute to a viable neutrality. However, there are new and emerging factors which need to be considered in studying the desirability and feasibility of a policy of neutrality in the context of contemporary international politics. This book presents three new factors—fixed and agreed-upon borders, no active involvement of trans-border non-state actors in the conflict, and cultural and ideological outlooks in favour of permanent neutrality—that are essential pre-conditions for a viable state of permanent neutrality today. The book aims to enrich the otherwise meagre contemporary IR literature on the subject and to explicate the major obstacles that would need to be overcome if Afghanistan were to make effective use of the policy of permanent neutrality in the future.

This book would have not been possible without the help of a number of gifted and caring individuals. I would like sincerely to thank Dr. William Maley, my academic advisor at the Asia Pacific College of Diplomacy (APCD) of the Australian National University, Dr. Amin Saikal, Dr. Nazif Shahrani, Dr. Rangin Dadfar Spanta, former Afghan Foreign Minister and National Security Advisor, Ambassador Mahmoud Saikal, Ambassador Eklil Hakimi, Ambassador Janan Mosazai, Ambassador Ashraf Haidari, and the Ambassadors of Austria, Switzerland, Sweden, and the Republic of Ireland in Canberra, Mr. Scott Smith at the United States Institute of Peace, and last but not least, Mrs. Nancy Dupree (who is no more amongst us) and her colleagues at the Afghanistan Center at Kabul University (ACKU) for sharing their insights and facilitating my research.

I am also deeply indebted to my wife and my best friend Jyotsna Hamida Andisha for her constant support and encouragement.

Acronyms

ANDSF	Afghanistan National Defence and Security Forces
ASEAN	Association of Southeast Asian Nations
CENTO	Central Treaty Organization
ETIM	East Turkestan Independence Movement
ICC	International Control Commission
IMU	Islamic Movement of Uzbekistan
ISAF	International Security Assistance Force
NAM	Non-alignment Movement
NATO	North Atlantic Treaty Organization
SEATO	The Southeast Asia Treaty Organization
SoFA	Status of Forces Agreement
UNAMA	United Nations Assistance Mission in Afghanistan
ZOPFAN	Zone of Peace, Freedom and Neutrality

Introduction

There is room in diplomacy for techniques designed to transform military stalemate into political stalemate. Neutralisation offers the possibility of such a transformation in some circumstances, especially wherein a minor state is the scene of domestic strife and competitive intervention.[1]

One of the most commonly used approaches in explaining states' behaviour in the modern international system suggests that to ensure their security interests, "states may either balance or bandwagon".[2] And when it comes to small and vulnerable states, Stephen Walt, a notable proponent of this approach, argues, "the weaker the state, the more likely it is to bandwagon rather than balance … Because weak states can do little to affect the outcome, and may suffer grievously in the process, they must choose the winning side".[3] This might be the best that international relations theory can offer in explaining the behaviour of states, but in reality it does not capture the whole range of options, from non-alignment to strategic autonomy, available to states operating in the international system. Rather, strategic and foreign policy decisions are made in an environment of interdependence and interaction, among various domestic and external factors and variables. Given these factors and variables, when a state is not in a position to either balance or bandwagon, it can seek to withdraw[4] from the conflict to ensure its own survival and independence. Neutrality, particularly of a permanent kind, is a classic policy for withdrawing from others' conflicts.

The concept of neutrality, defined as *non-participation in others' conflicts*, is as old as the notions of war and alliance. The most commonly quoted debate over the right to remain neutral is the Melian Dialogue of 416 BC, reported in Thucydides's *History of the Peloponnesian War*. The Melians attempted to distance themselves from the hostility between their powerful neighbours—the Athenians and the Spartans—arguing that by the law of nations they had the right to remain neutral, with no nation having the right to attack them without provocation. The Athenians swiftly rejected such a plea, on the grounds that the argument for neutrality was legally inconceivable and politically detrimental to the Athenian system of governance.[5]

As a foreign and security policy, neutrality is a relatively new phenomenon. It was conceived, along with the concept of the territorial state, during the Peace of Westphalia in 1648, but popularised only after the Congress of Vienna in 1815. However, only a small number of European states, such as Switzerland, Sweden, and later, Ireland, chose to adopt neutrality as their principal foreign policy, whilst for others, such as Belgium, Luxembourg, Austria, and to some extent, Finland, neutrality was imposed on them by their larger neighbours and outside powers. While its utility and sustainability as a comprehensive foreign and security policy have been a subject of debate amongst scholars of international politics, neutrality and neutralisation have remained a flexible instrument of statecraft in reducing tension and managing conflicts in the international system.

This study narrows its attention to the concept and practice of permanent neutrality. It draws on the well-known cases of permanent neutrality, such as Switzerland, Austria, and Laos (discussed in Chapter 3), in analysing the challenges and opportunities of permanent neutrality for candidate states and, in this case, for Afghanistan.

Scholars of international relations, such as Cyril Black, Efraim Karsh, Hanspeter Neuhold, and Cyrus French Wicker, have argued that neutrality—particularly permanent neutrality—offers an agreeable policy alternative to protracted conflict by removing small and often vulnerable states from areas that are contended for by the great powers, helping to reduce the likelihood of escalation and military confrontation amongst these powers. Since the advent of the territorial state, this diplomatic technique (that is, permanent neutrality/neutralisation) has frequently been recommended, though intermittently applied, to address the problems facing strategically located small and vulnerable states. Among the few countries to have applied permanent neutrality as an official state policy, Switzerland and Austria are considered success stories, whilst Belgium, Luxembourg, and Laos are cited as examples of failure. In cases such as Germany, the Koreas, Israel, Australia, and others, neutrality proposals never attracted serious attention and thus were not applied as state policy.

Afghanistan, as the main case study of this book, is an example of one such strategically situated, small state, where permanent neutrality has been proposed on a number of occasions. Throughout the nineteenth century, Afghanistan played the role of a buffer state separating the territories of the rival British and Russian empires in the region. Since regaining full independence in 1919—in particular, independence in making its own foreign policy—almost all rulers of Afghanistan have advocated some form of neutrality in their official policy statements.[6]

Afghanistan's tradition of neutrality/*bitarafi* is usually associated with an "Era of Tranquillity" from 1929 to 1978.[7] However, it is hard to ascertain whether this period of relative stability was a direct consequence of Afghanistan's policy of neutrality, or whether an environment of domestic and international stability enabled Afghan rulers to practise their own version of neutrality. The 1978 communist coup d'état and the subsequent Soviet military invasion disrupted that equilibrium and placed Afghanistan at the centre of East–West active hostility, triggering a cycle of violence and conflicts which continues to plague the country and the region to date.[8]

Various policy makers and scholars have argued that Afghanistan's return to neutrality will restore stability and tranquillity in the country. Hence in the past four decades attempts have been made to turn Afghanistan into a permanently neutral state.

Afghanistan's neutrality efforts and proposals, 1980–2014

In Afghanistan, neutrality keeps emerging as an ad hoc solution for the restoration of security and balance of power in the region. Most of the neutralisation efforts and proposals have been initiated by outside powers, often during situations of crisis or toward the end of foreign interventions in the country.

One of the first attempts to apply "permanent neutrality" as a possible solution to the crises in Afghanistan was a US-supported,[9] British-led neutralisation initiative in the immediate aftermath of the Soviet military invasion of Afghanistan. The initiative was put forward by the British Foreign Secretary, Lord Carrington, in the midst of international fury over the invasion. It envisaged that an agreement on the neutralisation of Afghanistan, modelled after the 1955 agreement on the neutralisation of Austria,[10] could end the Soviet military occupation and pave the way for a face-saving withdrawal of the Soviet forces from Afghanistan.[11] The initiative, which included an immediate withdrawal of Soviet forces, was swiftly rejected by the Soviet leadership and the communist regime in Kabul on the grounds that it was a plot by the West to undo the "revolution" and re-establish Western influence in Afghanistan.[12]

The next attempt to neutralise and even demilitarise Afghanistan came in the wake of the Soviet military withdrawal from Afghanistan in 1988. This time the initiative was conceived in Moscow, though it was officially proposed by the regime in Kabul. President Najibullah (1987–1992) called on the Secretary General of the UN to hold an international conference on Afghanistan to discuss the reinstatement and confirmation of Afghanistan's permanent neutrality and to work out an international assistance programme in support of a peace and reconciliation programme.[13] On the domestic level, Najibullah instructed Afghanistan's Academy of Science to study the feasibility of adopting a policy of demilitarised permanent neutrality. A year later, in May 1990, the Constitution was amended to reflect the regime's desire for neutralisation and demilitarisation. An entire new chapter in the amended constitution was dedicated to foreign policy and for the first time in the country's history, the term "permanent neutrality" featured in its constitution.[14]

Although Najibullah managed to secure consensus among the elites supporting his regime on the declaration of a demilitarised and permanently neutral status, this initiative hardly attracted any serious support at the regional and international level. The Western capitals and the Afghan resistance forces, the "Mujahideen", were predicting an imminent collapse of the Kabul regime soon after the withdrawal of the Soviet forces.[15] They perceived the neutralisation initiative to be an attempt by the regime to assure its survival beyond the Soviet departure. Besides, at that juncture, when the Soviet Union was on the verge of collapse, neither Kabul nor Moscow had enough political capital to garner wider support for such an ambitious proposal.

The failure of both initiatives, the West's in the early 1980s and the Soviet's support in 1989, indicate that, as long as any of the conflicting parties believe that a victory is achievable on the battlefield, accepting neutrality as the basis for a solution to a protracted conflict was out of the question. Hence, creating consensus among external and internal stakeholders on neutrality declaration requires a military stalemate accompanied by diplomatic leverage and perseverance.

After the failure of Lord Carrington's initiative in the early 1980s, Selig Harrison, an American scholar and South Asia expert, opined that a "Finland-style arrangement",[16] in other words a softer and more Soviet-friendly version of neutralisation, which could include a phased withdrawal of Soviet forces, with a medium-term return to Afghanistan's policy of *bitarafi*, could win Moscow's acceptance.[17] Harrison believed that such an arrangement was possible only if the Soviet Union pursued limited objectives in Afghanistan, and if the leadership in Moscow was serious about finding a consensus to the conflict in Afghanistan rather than relying on the total victory of its client government there. This hypothesis turned out to be false.

Another noted but non-official appeal came at the height of the Taliban and Al Qaeda's reign of terror in Afghanistan. Peter Tomsen, former US envoy for the Afghan resistance, in a June 2000 hearing before the US Senate Committee on Foreign Relations,[18] urged the US Government to encourage and support international negotiations aimed at removing Afghanistan from regional rivalries. Similar to Carrington's suggestion in 1980, Tomsen proposed that the "1955 State Treaty on Austrian Neutrality can function as a useful model for neutralization of Afghanistan".[19] However, the administrations of both President Bill Clinton and President George W. Bush had no visible foreign policy interest in Afghanistan during the 1990s and paid no attention to Tomsen's neutralisation proposal.

During nearly a decade-long intensive US-led foreign military presence in Afghanistan following the 9/11 attacks on US soil by Afghanistan-based groups, the only country which occasionally spoke about the restoration of Afghanistan's neutrality was the Russian Federation. The Russian government, while supporting the international security and reconstruction efforts, emphasised that Afghanistan should become a neutral state after the International Security Assistant Forces (ISAF) mission ended. Russia actively campaigned for the removal of the North Atlantic Treaty Organization (NATO)/ISAF hubs from the former Soviet Republics in Central Asia. Russian officials in private meetings with the Afghan authorities continuously raised their concern about the size, purpose, and duration of the US military bases inside Afghanistan.[20] Thus the Russian policy of favouring a neutral Afghanistan followed the old pattern in the context of the great power rivalry where the weaker power, in this case Russia, usually prefers neutralisation of the contested area as a mean to prevent rivals from access and domination in the area.

Discussions on neutrality-based solutions resumed in the wake of President Obama's plan to withdraw US forces from Afghanistan. In a 2009 *New York Times* op-ed, former US Assistant Secretary of State Karl Inderfurth and Ambassador James Dobbins, who later became President Obama's special envoy for Afghanistan and Pakistan, opined that the "ultimate exit strategy" for Afghanistan could include a multilateral accord to declare Afghanistan a permanently neutral country.[21] In a report called "Afghan Peace Talks",[22] Dobbins insisted on Afghanistan's permanent neutrality although he used the term *permanently non-aligned* in order to not upset President Karzai[23]—as a requisite of a durable solution for the conflict in Afghanistan.

In a private testimony to the Senate Foreign Relations Committee on 23 June 2011, former Secretary of State Hillary Clinton confirmed the need for a broad regional diplomatic gathering akin to that of the Congress of Vienna in 1815, which had declared "the Benelux countries as a free zone".[24] She argued that "if we could get to that point with the regional powers in South Asia that would not recommence with the great game in Afghanistan that would be a very worthy outcome".[25] Officially, however, neutrality remained an unmarketable policy, in part due to President Karzai's resistance to the idea. Instead, the concept of a grand regional gathering was converted into a regional confidence building and cooperation forum among Afghanistan and its neighbours, known as the Istanbul Process, launched in November 2011.[26]

The most recent call for neutralisation came after Afghanistan signed Strategic Partnership Agreements (SPA's) with the United States and a number of other major regional and European countries and subsequently became a "major non-NATO ally" of the United States.[27] Audrey Kurth Cronin, Professor of Public Policy at George Mason University, argued in 2013 that "a tradition of repelling invaders … as well as formidable geography that is difficult to occupy make Afghanistan a natural candidate for neutralization".[28] Given the regional and international security implications of Afghanistan's destabilisation, Cronin insisted that building consensus on declaring Afghanistan a neutral state would be more viable in a post-US/NATO withdrawal environment than at any time during the Cold War.

Afghanistan's neutrality was also discussed in a regional Track Two forum recently established to develop policy recommendations for confidence building and closer cooperation among the countries in the region. This resulted, in November 2013, in a *Joint Declaration on Regional Peace and Stability*, recommending a gradual "Afghan led and Afghan specific neutrality".[29] The declaration described neutrality as "a vision and goal" to be arrived at gradually and in tandem with other regional initiatives elaborated in the declaration.

In a nutshell, the new advocates of neutralisation believe that a formal and internationally sanctioned treaty of neutrality can re-align regional and international interests, ensuring security and stability in Afghanistan after the withdrawal of the NATO/ISAF forces. However, the lack of considerable national debates on the permanent neutrality of Afghanistan in the past 18 years conveys a different message.

Given the above analysis, it is evident that the subject of Afghanistan's neutrality/*bitarafi*, though not comprehensively studied, re-surfaces every now and then in regional and international discourse on Afghanistan as a possible compromise option for returning to stability and maintaining regional security.

The overarching issue with which this book is concerned, while analysing permanent neutrality as a state policy particularly in the case of Afghanistan, is this: under what circumstances can permanent neutrality be applied, and what are the main ingredients of success, and the causes of failure, in applying permanent neutrality. Understanding these two circumstances or factors, in turn, offers a reliable framework for analysing the feasibility and desirability of permanent neutrality in Afghanistan.

The book does not engage in analysing the possible relationship between Afghanistan's neutrality and its relative stability in the past, since the author believes that a combination of different factors and not necessarily neutrality alone contributed to the relative stability and tranquillity that existed in Afghanistan prior to 1978.

Methodology

This book utilises conceptual and historical analysis within the qualitative approach as its methodological framework for examining the concept of neutrality, and in particular, neutralisation in the context of a state's foreign and security policy.

The book does not follow a "structured and focused case comparison" model of inquiry; the three well-known cases of permanent neutrality, namely, Switzerland, Austria, and Laos, are used to illustrate the examples of success and failure in regard to a policy of permanent neutrality. The motive for choosing only these three countries stems from the existence of certain similarities that these countries share with Afghanistan—the main subject of this study. Like Afghanistan, these three countries are landlocked countries, and at the time of declaring their neutrality, they were surrounded by powerful and hostile neighbours. Ultimately, adopting neutrality was seen, particularly in the cases of Austria and Laos, as an externally driven consensus solution for ending conflict and occupation.

Limitations

The study of neutrality in general faces many theoretical and analytical challenges and limitations and this book is not an exception. The sample size of permanently neutral states is very small in comparison to, for example, allied states or non-aligned states. Even within this small sample, characteristic variations across permanently neutral states are rich enough to make each country a distinctive case study, thus making generalisation an even more difficult task. However, the examination of neutralised states allows one to identify certain features, rules, and obligations common across all permanently neutral states, enabling scholars to suggest a number of geographic, material, social, and indigenous factors, which could substantially determine the success or failure of neutralisation.[30] These factors will be taken into account in examining the challenges Afghanistan and other states desiring to become or remain neutral have to face.

Another challenge this study faces emanates from the fact that all major previous studies of the possibility of neutralisation of states were conducted in the context of Cold War hostilities, whereas the current discussion of neutrality is a novel case and in the context of a renewed great powers' rivalry in Eastern Europe, Central Asia, and the Middle East. These regions which presumed to be within Russia's traditional sphere of influence,[31] and China's newly extended economic and security interest zone,[32] are in fact hosting US and NATO military forces.

In addition to its unique feature of being a post-Cold War study of neutrality in general and Afghanistan's neutrality in particular the book makes one further contribution to the discourse on neutralisation in the case of Muslim majority states by incorporating the views of Islamic international law (Siyar). Given the recent trend in re-Islamisation of Muslim societies and states, this debate is highly significant particularly while discussing the feasibility and desirability of the permanent neutrality of Afghanistan, an Islamic Republic surrounded by majority Muslim states; a discussion of the place of neutrality in the context of "Siyar" constitutes a worthwhile contribution to knowledge in the subject.

Notes

1 Cyril E. Black et al., *Neutralization and World Politics* (Princeton: Princeton University Press, 1968), p. vi.
2 Stephen M. Walt, *The Origins of Alliances* (Ithaca: Cornell University Press, 1987), p. 114.
3 Ibid, p. 114.
4 According to Wei Zongyou, beside balancing and bandwagoning, states have a third option of withdrawing. Zongyou in the context of the struggle between hegemons argues that "middling and small powers that have no interest in this conflict are likely follow the withdrawing strategy, so as to ensure their own survival and independence". See Wei Zongyou, "In the Shadow of Hegemony: Strategic Choices", *Chinese Journal of International Politics*, 1 (2006): 195–229.
5 Thucydides, *The Peloponnesian War* (New York: Random House, 1951), p. 332. Available from: http://nku.edu/~weirk/ir/melian.html.
6 Amin Saikal, *Modern Afghanistan: A History of Struggle and Survival* (London: I. B. Tauris, 2006), p. 123.
7 Audrey Kurth Cronin, "Thinking Long on Afghanistan: Could It Be Neutralized?" *The Washington Quarterly*, 36(1) (2013): 55.
8 Abdul Samad Ghaus, *The Fall of Afghanistan: An Insider's Account* (New York, London: Brassey's Ltd); 1st edition, January 1988, p. 209.
9 "Carter Backs Afghan Neutrality", *Sarasota Herald-Tribune*, 27 February 1980, p. 1.
10 Carrington emphasised that "we have the idea of neutralization in a broad form, but there are certain paths we could follow". See Ibid.
11 Edith Hassman, "U.S. Foreign Policy: The Views from Vienna", *Executive Intelligence Review*, 7(10) (11 March 1980): 56.
12 "Britain Gets Private Word on Afghanistan", *Sarasota Herald-Tribune*, 12 March 1980, p. 3.

13 "Permanent Neutrality and Disarmament of Afghanistan", collection of articles from a seminar held by the Academy of Science of Afghanistan. Government Publication, 1989, p. 3

14 The preamble read "creating favourable conditions for determining the legal status of permanent neutrality of Afghanistan and its demilitarization". See, the Constitution of Afghanistan 1990, available at: http://afghan-web.com/history/const/const1990.html

15 "USSR: Withdrawal from Afghanistan" Director of Central Intelligence, Special National Intelligence Estimate, March 1988, p. 219. Available at: https://cia.gov /library.

16 After losing parts of its territory to Soviet Union during the Winter War (1939–1940) and a new attack during the Second World War, Finland signed an Agreement of Friendship, Cooperation, and Mutual Assistance with the Soviet Union in April 1948. Despite restrictions and costs, Finland remained outside great power conflicts by adopting a policy of neutrality; the country did not participate in the Marshall Plan, took neutral positions on Soviet actions abroad, stayed away from NATO, and successfully resisted Soviet pressure for cooperating with the Warsaw Pact. See Brian S. Faloon, "Aspects of Finnish Neutrality", *Irish Studies in International Affairs*, 1(3) (1982): 3–12.

17 Selig S. Harrison, "Dateline Afghanistan: Exit through Finland?" *Foreign Policy*, 41 (Winter 1980–1981): 183.

18 The Taliban: Engagement or Confrontation?, Hearing before the U.S. Senate, Committee on Foreign Relations. 20 June 2000.

19 Peter Tomsen, "Chance for Peace in Afghanistan, the Taliban's Days Are Numbered", *Foreign Affairs*, 79(1) (January–February 2000): 182, 179–182.

20 Author's discussion and interview with former senior Afghan security officials in Kabul and Canberra, August–September 2013. See, Nasir A. Andisha, "Neutrality in Afghanistan's Foreign Policy", Special Report, the United States Institute of Peace, March 2015, p.12.

21 Karl F. Inderfurth and James Dobbins, "Ultimate Exit Strategy", *The New York Times*, 26 March 2009. Available at: http://nytimes.com/2009/03/27/opinion/27 iht-edinderfurth.html.

22 James Shinn and James Dobbins, *Afghan Peace Talk: A Primer* (RAND Corporation, 2011). Available at: http://rand.org/pubs/monographs/MG1131.h tml.

23 In his conversation with Western diplomats, President Karzai objected to their use of the term *neutrality* in reference to Afghanistan's future international status.

24 Daniel Dombey and Matthew Green, "US Aims to Turn Afghanistan into Neutral Zone", *The Financial Times*, 27 June 2011.

25 Ibid.

26 The Istanbul Process: http://mfa.gov.af/en/news/4598.

27 "Major non-NATO ally" is a title given by the US Government under Section 2350a(f)(2) of Title 10, United States Code to strategically important allies who are not members of the North Atlantic Treaty Organization. See, http://globalsecurity.org/military/agency/dod/mnna.htm.

28 Audrey Kurth Cronin, "Thinking Long on Afghanistan: Could it be Neutralized?" *The Washington Quarterly*, 36(1) (2013): 56.

29 "Afghanistan's Region: 2014 & Beyond", Joint Declaration on regional Peace and Stability. 17 November 2013.

30 Nicholas Mercuro and Alan T. Leonhard, *Neutrality: Changing Concepts and Practices* (New Orleans, LA: University Press of America, 1988), pp. 131–134.
31 See Irina Zviagel'skia, "Russia and Central Asia: Problem of Security", ed. Boris Z. Rumer, *Central Asia at the End of the Transition* (New York, London: M.E. Sharpe Armonk, 2005), p. 80.
32 Richard Weitz, "Beijing Braces for Afghanistan 2014" (January 2014). Available at: http://chinausfocus.com/foreign-policy/beijing-braces-for-afghanistan-2014/.

1 Definitions, types, and evolution of the concept and practice of neutrality

Neutrality is simply defined as "the state of not supporting or helping either side in a conflict".[1] The rights and duties of neutral states and persons were formally defined and codified by the Hague Conventions of 1907.[2] In the context of international law, neutrality is a wartime political position involving legal duties and responsibilities and:

> observance of a strict and honest impartiality, so as not to afford advantage in the war to either party; and particularly in so far restraining its trade to the accustomed course which is held in time of peace, as not to render assistance to one of the belligerents in escaping the effects of the other's hostilities. Even a loan of money to one of the belligerent parties is considered a violation of neutrality.[3]

The definition of neutrality also places certain obligations on belligerents, such as not violating the territorial integrity of neutral states and avoiding the use of neutrals' territory as a base for any sort of hostile activities against each other. However, in practice, particularly during the First World War, violation of Belgian and Grecian neutrality by Germany and Italy reduced the credibility of the status of neutrality and placed the burden of self-defence on the shoulders of neutral states, thus popularizing the concept of armed neutrality.

While traditional legal definitions focus mainly on the negative rights and duties of neutrals during war (that is, what they should not do), subsequent definitions presented by Oppenheim and Lawrence[4] provide a more positive and constructive role for the neutral state. For example, a neutral state was defined as an honest brokerage capable of offering good offices and having the potential to mediate between the belligerents. Hence, in its contemporary use, neutrality is not only a wartime legal status but also a peacetime political and diplomatic posture.

Types of neutrality

Like many other concepts in international relations (IR), the scope and nature of neutrality have evolved, and various types and brands of neutrality have emerged.[5] Neutrality's definition has been stretched to accommodate the interests of states and changes in global politics. Labels, such as "neutralisation", "neutralism", "armed neutrality", "positive neutrality", "non-aligned", "military non-aligned", "non-allied", and so on, are used to describe states' foreign and security policies with different degrees of neutrality.

Based on their legal and political dimensions, the policies of neutrality, in general, have been divided into the following three broad categories:

1. Neutralisation or permanent neutrality
2. Neutralism or non-alignment
3. Neutrality or military un-aligned

Each type of neutrality has its own features and characteristics and can be further divided into sub-categories depending on the depth of analysis one undertakes. This study focuses mostly on the first type, that is, neutralisation; however, the definitions of all three major categories of neutrality are provided.

1. *Neutralisation or permanent neutrality* is the formal and strict type of neutrality practised during both war and peace. Permanent neutrality could be either self-declared or externally prescribed and enforced, in which case it is mostly referred to as *neutralisation*.[6] Switzerland's neutrality serves as a classic example of the former, whilst Belgium, Luxembourg, Austria, and Laos are instances of the latter type.
    Cronin defines neutralisation as:

    > a reciprocal agreement between a small, strategically located weak state and two or more major powers at odds with each other. It is an interest-based tool, designed to keep enemies from directly confronting each other over a territory whose strategic significance affects them all. Neutralisation is not about building neighbourly harmony, it's about avoiding major war.[7]

    Hence neutralisation is also referred to as a policy of permanent neutrality, with a neutralised state being:

    > A state whose political independence and territorial integrity is guaranteed permanently by a collective agreement of great powers,

subject to conditions that the neutralized state will not take up arms against another state, except to defend itself, and will not assume treaty obligations which may compromise its neutralized status.[8]

While cognisant of the technical difference, this research uses the terms *neutralisation* and *permanent neutrality* interchangeably. The existence of an official and internationally recognised agreement distinguishes permanent neutrality from other types of neutrality.

2. *Neutralism* is a Cold War phenomenon and refers to a policy of distancing oneself from the East–West conflict. Neutralism, in the eyes of its proponents (mainly the Third World), was an attempt to "remove or, at least, mitigate some of the harshness of the Cold War struggle".[9] Based on this definition, neutralism could be synonymous with non-alignment and peaceful coexistence. At its essence, neutralism is a political and diplomatic posture and has no legal implications for a state adopting this policy. Non-aligned nations argued that staying aloof from the superpowers' conflict did not mean being indifferent toward injustices and suffering; rather it allowed them to have an independent outlook toward global issues.

3. *Neutral or militarily un-aligned* refers to the traditional form of neutrality enshrined in the provisions of international law and often observed during inter-state wars. Neutral states not only adhere to the legal obligations of neutrality during a war but also stay militarily un-aligned during peacetime at their own discretion. In most cases, neutral states declare their peacetime neutrality through some form of internal legislation. Throughout much of the twentieth century, Sweden, Ireland, and Finland were often described as neutral states.

Neutrality in theory

As neutrality is a multi-dimensional concept, one has to borrow insights from different approaches in IR to build a reasonably inclusive theoretical framework for its explanation. While neutrality is a historical concept, there is no single dominant theory of IR or framework of analysis to guide the study of the concept or its various forms. Agius argues that "neutrality predates key concepts such as the state, sovereignty and anarchy but it is largely sidelined in theorising".[10] In terms of theoretical work, neutrality seems like a no man's land in the middle of rich and burgeoning IR disciplines of security and foreign policy studies. Much like the instances of neutrality, its study is confined mostly to Europe, particularly to Nordic countries.

The discipline of IR examines the dynamics of interactions between sovereign states and other entities within the international system.[11] Since neutrality is one type of inter-state relationship, albeit an uncommon one, scholars have attempted to explain neutrality from the perspectives of different theories and paradigms of IR and its sub-fields, such as security and foreign policy studies. By reviewing the three major IR paradigms of realism, liberalism, and constructivism, and drawing on insights from Islamic public and international law, this chapter attempts to locate the concept of neutrality within IR literature.

Neutrality and realism

It is believed that realism and neutrality share a common historical origin. IR scholars such as Bauslaugh,[12] Agius and Devine,[13] and Jan Martin Rolence[14] suggest that the first written record of debate on the practice of neutrality goes back to the same Melian Dialogue in Thucydides's *History of the Peloponnesian War*, which realism cherishes as setting the "maxim of power". Hence, the phenomenon of neutrality was either ignored or sidelined in the past as it was considered an immoral and weak position.

However, realist theories fell short of offering a credible theoretical explanation for the concept of neutrality. For example, classical realism discards the notion of neutrality, as it is contrary to realism's fundamental principles, such as anarchy and the need for maximising a state's security by increasing power and capabilities.

On the other hand, the neo-realist theory advanced by Kenneth Waltz, among others, which focuses on the structure of the international system and a state's survival, finds the concept of neutrality to be amenable to the tenet of realism. While neo-realism in its essence is a theory of great powers' behaviour, Waltz's concept of "relative power", and his assertion that understanding a state's behaviour is related to the share of each state's capability, offers a rationalist explanation for the behaviour of neutral states.[15]

Neo-realist theory contends that neutrality is a rational policy option for small states to survive in an anarchical system. Altfeld and De Mesquita applied a rational actor model to justify a state's choice of remaining neutral in hostilities, concluding that, "at least during times of war, the rational actor approach provides useful insights into the likely action of a third state".[16]

Notwithstanding the fact that some aspects of neutrality defy the core principles of the realist theory,[17] realism certainly is an instructive point from which to begin one's inquiry into the subject of neutrality. This is the case since as a theory of power politics, realism can help explain the existence and evolution of neutrality as a rational wartime foreign and security policy for small states. However, the presence of neutral states after the end of the Cold War, and during a period of rapid European integration in the

1990s, demanded an alternative and more responsive approach to the understanding of neutrality: something that realism failed to deliver.

Neutrality and liberalism

Given the more interventionist and activist nature of liberal theories, this school of thought hardly offers any plausible theoretical framework for explaining the concept of neutrality. The self-isolationists' notion of neutrality is, in fact, incompatible with the tenets of liberal ideas such as democratic peace, collective security, and international justice. Rolence argues that "the inter-war idealism, inspired by the idea of an international cosmopolitan moral order as described by Kant in the Perpetual Peace, saw neutrality in conflict with the 'harmony of interests' of all states and the principle of 'collective security' which were supposed to underpin the post-WW1 international order".[18]

In an attempt to connect neutrality to liberal internationalism, scholars such as Hersch Lauterpacht, Efraim Karsh, Neal G. Jesse, and Laurent Goetschel, each in separate articles, have suggested that neutrality, collective security, and international cooperation are not mutually exclusive concepts.[19] For example, Jesse insists that neoliberalism offers the best theoretical framework for explaining the dynamics of Irish neutrality. He argues that the Irish policy of neutrality is grounded on domestic values, moral principles, Irish identity, and norms such as self-determination and sovereignty, and "[n]eutrality is thus a means by which a state can assert its sovereignty vis-à-vis the international order. From this standpoint neutrality is a legitimate and appropriate form of behaviour".[20]

In a rebuttal to Jesse's argument, Karen Devine has argued that when principles such as identities and domestic opinions are the main determinants of the Irish policy of neutrality, then "critical social constructivism provides a more nuanced understanding of Irish neutrality than the neoliberal framework suggested by Jesse".[21]

Notwithstanding the aforementioned attempts to explain neutrality through neo-realist or neoliberal lenses, in its essence, neutrality largely challenges the foundational concepts of these theories, such as anarchy and collective security.

Since neo-realism and neoliberal explanations focus mainly on the exogenous determinants of neutrality, such as self-determination, protection of sovereignty, and state survival, while leaving the endogenous factors of states' policies unattended, Christine Agius rightly emphasises that "a reliance on realist and idealist approaches provides only limited analytical framework for understanding neutrality".[22]

In order better to comprehend the influence of internal factors, such as national identity, norms, and values, on the behaviour of neutral states, and to acquire a more contemporary worldview of the study of international relations, it is essential at this stage to turn to a constructivist approach to the study of inter-state relations.

Neutrality and constructivism

The existence of neutrality after the end of bipolarity could be better explained by constructivist theory. Recent research on European neutrals suggests that socially constructed values, ideas, and identities are the major determinants of a state's behaviour. Karen Devine asserts that independence and identity are the key factors in explaining Irish neutrality; empirical evidence gathered from data based on public opinion supports a "critical social constructivist framework of understanding of Irish neutrality".[23]

Agius argues that Sweden's neutrality has a strong normative foundation, with there being an inherent connection between neutrality and Swedish identity, as "neutrality has played a substantive part in constructing nation-state identity and actions both internally and externally".[24]

Laurant Goetschel calls neutrality a "principled belief", arguing that "the function of neutrality is better understood by looking briefly at the role of identity and beliefs in International Relations".[25] When values, interests, and ideas form the core of a nation's political identity, Goetschel further asserts that "neutrality has a role as an identity-provider for the population".[26]

The above review vindicates the argument that no single IR theory could alone explain the concept of neutrality; however, the review also shows that among the major schools of IR, the neo-realist branch of realism better explains the motives and intentions of strategically placed small states opting for neutrality, while constructivism offers a framework for understanding the reasons why states continue to maintain and preserve their neutrality at the time of peace.

The realist approach attaches great importance to state capability and resources in determining a state's foreign policy behaviour. Therefore, the choice of neutrality for this school is directly linked to a state's capability and resources, or lack thereof. On the other hand, for liberals, neutrality, similar to other foreign and security policy positions, is largely shaped by the attitudes and actions of individuals or groups, institutional constraints, societal values, and identities. The contemporary literature on neutrality, however, uses constructivist approaches to explain the existence of a neutral state and its relevance in a post-Cold War order. Hence one can conclude that a combination (synthesis) of neo-realist and constructivist approaches presents a more robust basis for a theoretical examination of neutrality and is as such considered throughout this study.

Neutrality in Islam

Neutrality was looked upon as an irrelevant and even immoral concept in the early Christian thought, particularly after the introduction of the Just War doctrine by Saint Augustine. Scant deliberation on neutrality often featured at the margins of debates on just and unjust war among Christian clergy and kings. Without any prejudice to the importance of neutrality's place in other religions theology and political literature, this research focuses on the feasibility and desirability of the permanent neutrality of Afghanistan (a conservative Muslim state surrounded by majority Muslim states, except China) and evaluates neutrality's place in "Siyar",[27] or Islamic International Law, and inter-state relations in Islam.

As signatories of the UN charter, Muslim states are subject to many rules of public international law. However, the heavy influence of Shariáh law and the presence of powerful Islamist constituencies in majority Muslim states makes it imperative that grand policies either be compatible with, or at least not contradict, the teachings of Islam.

Similar to mainstream IR and public international law, Islamic law research on neutrality, particularly in its contemporary connotation, is limited to the writings of a handful of Muslim scholars. Mohammad Hamidullah,[28] Majid Khadduri,[29] Muhammad Abu Zahra,[30] Wahba al-Zuhayli,[31] and Anke Bouzenita[32] are the main scholars who have written on the subject of neutrality in the Islamic polity.[33] Moreover, IR scholars, such as Efraim Karsh[34] and David Brackett,[35] have also made some (at best simplistic) references to Islam's supposedly hostile attitude toward neutrality. Hamidullah, one of the earliest writers to discuss neutrality specifically, offers a detailed account of the practice of neutrality, its nuances, and references to it found in traditional sources from the earlier Islamic period. He traces the practice of neutrality in the conduct of the city-state of Madina in relation to its neighbouring non-Muslim tribes, the existence of neutral factions during the first internal war among the Muslim leadership (the First Fitna 656–661), and finally the treaties of non-aggression between Muslim rulers and non-Muslim states and territories. Hamidullah argues that the Arabic word *i'tizal* (isolation and keeping away), which is used frequently in the Qur'an and Hadith, is the predecessor of the term *al-heyad*, which means neutrality in modern Arabic. Quoting examples and referring to passages from the Qur'an and Hadith, Hamidullah emphasises that "the notion and the fact of neutrality were not unknown to early Muslims. [However]

… the Muslim jurists do not treat the question in a separate chapter, but describe its provisions partly in the laws of peace and partly in the laws of war".[36] While Hamidullah admits the under-developed status of the legality of neutrality within Islamic polity and refrains from providing a definitive statement on the subject, Majid Khadduri, a prominent scholar of Islamic law, believes that in classical Islamic theory, there is no room for such a thing as a policy of neutrality. He argues that "if neutrality is taken to mean the attitude of a state, which voluntarily desires to keep out of war by not taking sides, no such status is recognised in the Muslim legal theory. For Islam must *ipso jure* be at war with any state that refuses to come to terms with it either by submitting to Muslim rule or by accepting temporary peace agreement".[37]

While Hamidullah and Khadduri have explained their interpretation of the concept of neutrality from the classical perspective, scholars such as Abu Zahra and Zuhayli take a more pragmatic approach toward the subject of neutrality. In the classical view, the world is divided into Dar Al-Islam (world of Islam) and Dar Al-Harb (world of war). According to this view, and based on the interpretation by classical Muslim scholars of verses within Chapter 9 (at-taubah) of the Qur'an,[38] "[a]rmed Jihad is to be carried out until all lands are liberated from unbelievers and when all unbelievers submit to the rule of Islam".[39]

However, Abu Zahra and Zuhayli, among other modern scholars, challenge the classical dual division of the world into Dar Al-Islam and Dar Al-Harb. Abu Zahra suggests that there exists a middle ground between the two "worlds" or realms, and he calls it Dar Al-Hayad (realm of neutrality or truce). Abu Zahra enforces his theory of "middle ground" with reference to Verse 90 of Chapter 4 in the Qur'an,[40] arguing "that the Qur'an allows the existence of third parties who neither want to fight the Muslims, nor their enemy".[41]

Likewise, Zuhayli accepts the existence of the provision of neutrality in Islamic law on the grounds that the dual division of the world into the realm of Islam and the realm of war by some Islamic scholars is a purely pragmatic division influenced by the political situation of the time. He further argues, "Islam recognised what resembles the contemporary forms of neutrality as a political reality, if not as a juristic system, in a way comparable to its beginnings in Europe. There is, however, no obstacle in recognising neutrality as a legal system".[42] These groups of scholars have referred to Islam's special relations and peace agreements with the rulers of Abyssinia (Ethiopia), Nubia, and Cyprus as historical evidence for the existence of some form of neutrality during the time of the Prophet Mohammed and his companions.[43]

Outside the Islamic scholars' debate on neutrality, Efraim Karsh and David S. Brackett have made references to Islam's attitude toward the practice of neutrality. These scholars have quoted part of the last sentence of Verse 74, Chapter 4 of the Qur'an, which says that "Allah will afflict them with a painful doom in the world and the Hereafter, and they have no protecting friend nor helper in the earth"[44] to argue that Islam detests neutrality and neutrals. The verse, the last sentence of which is partly quoted by the two authors, in fact discusses the events surrounding the Expedition of Tabuk in 630 AD. The word "them" in the verse specifically refers to a group of "hypocrites" who travelled along with Prophet Mohammed to Tabuk. Hypocrites,[45] their deeds and characters have been explored in detail in Chapter 63, Surat Al-Munāfiqūn (The Hypocrites), in the Qur'an. While Karsh has attempted, rather without scholarly rigour, to elide the difference between hypocrites and neutrals and has argued that whom Prophet Mohammed used to call hypocrites were in fact neutrals,[46] Brackett has simply disregarded the difference between the two terms and has added the word *neutrals* in brackets in front of the word *them* in his quotation from the Qur'an.

Notwithstanding the misconstruction on the part of Karsh and Brackett, there seems to be a general consensus among contemporary scholars about the recognition and practices of neutrality in the earlier Islamic period. However, whether it is permissible for an Islamic polity to adopt neutrality as its official state policy is an open-ended debate. For example, from a broader Sharia perspective neutrality is not acceptable in case a war arises between a Muslim and a non-Muslim state, particularly when the aggression is initiated by the non-Muslim state. Moreover, neutrality is not advisable in case of brazen repression against a weak state, particularly when the remaining neutral jeopardises Muslim unity. More importantly, neutrality is considered a temporary status, normally for a maximum of 10 years or until it serves a state's interest. Hence, accepting or declaring permanent neutrality, as argued by Bouzenita, "defy the purpose of *da'wah*[47] and cannot, therefore, be condoned".[48]

On the other hand, there is sufficient textual and historical evidence brought forth by modern scholars in support of the permissibility of some forms of neutrality in Islam, although not the permanent type.[49] While this historical evidence points to the practice of temporary neutrality in the earlier Islamic period, under Islamic law, the concept of neutrality has not been further developed into a separate legal and political system. One can still conclude that Islam takes a pragmatic approach toward neutrality, condoning adapting neutrality on a temporary basis when it is in the interest of a Muslim polity (Table 1.1).

Table 1.1 A summary of the main theoretical approaches toward neutrality

Schools of IR	Aspects Emphasised	Explanations of neutrality
1. Realism		
Classical realism	Anarchy, power maximisation, capability, and resources	A by-product of balance of power, not prudent policy
Neo-realism	Relative power, state survival	As a rational choice for small and geographically buffer states to protect sovereignty
2. Liberalism		
Classical-liberalism, idealism	Values, principles, norms, collective peace harmony, and cooperation	Neutrality linked to domestic values and moral principles
Liberal internationalism		
Institutionalism	Collective security, international cooperation, and democratic peace	Neutrality hinders collective security and international cooperation
3. Constructivism		
Critical-social constructivism	Identity, beliefs, and values, not anarchy but socially constructed ideas	Neutrality provides identity and norm of behaviour for nation-states

Functions of neutralisation

Scholars and policymakers have described neutralisation and permanent neutrality as a *flexible instrument of statecraft*, a remedy for removing the causes of war, a diplomatic technique to transform military stalemates into political stalemates, and finally, a by-product of the balance of power or a catalyst for strengthening it. In general, at the macro level, neutralisation is a policy instrument for the management of power in the international system, whilst at the micro level, it is the least bad choice for small and weak states to avoid war and preserve their sovereignty. According to Black, neutralisation has three primary functions: (1) removing or insulating an area from active hostilities among the great powers; (2) preventing exacerbation of conflict in zones of great powers' contention and rivalry; and (3) ending active conflict aided by external powers, particularly when neither side is capable of an outright victory.

Black summarises the main functions of permanent neutrality as *conflict moderation*, *conflict avoidance*, and *conflict termination*, which fit into the context of neutralisation as a tool of conflict management in the international system.[50] However, in the context of the foreign and security policies of small states, permanent neutrality also offers a rational policy choice for small states to survive in a situation of anarchy by remaining detached from another's war. If successfully upheld and preserved, neutrality could also function as a source of state identity and provide good offices for conflict mediation. In a nutshell, as an alternative to active conflict, permanent neutrality serves the interest of both the great powers concerned with the stability of the international system and the small states striving to preserve their sovereignty and territorial integrity.

Permanent neutrality variables

Before dealing with the questions of *when* and *how* permanent neutrality is applicable and sustainable, it is necessary to remember that permanent neutrality is not an ideal foreign policy option that states would like to adopt in normal circumstances. According to Karsh "the decision by a state to adopt a policy of permanent neutrality is not always a matter of free choice".[51] It is a compromise solution, applicable only to certain areas and in certain circumstances. Likewise, Black stresses that "[n]eutralization is relevant primarily to geographically definable areas in which two or more external actors have substantial and competitive interest".[52] Geographically definable areas could include cities, waterways, and outer space; however, this research focuses only on states as the main subject of neutralisation. Hence, our conjecture is that a policy of permanent neutrality is applicable in a sub-system when a small and, usually, weak state is located in an area of competitive interest of two or more major states. This description teases out three main characteristics of a state suitable for neutralisation:

1. Geography: Neutrals or candidate states are located in an area of major power conflict and usually act as a buffer or insulator.
2. Capabilities: Neutrals or candidate states are weak and small and not major players in international politics.
3. Stalemate: The surrounding states have competitive interests inside the neutral or candidate state, but a complete domination by any one state is not likely.

Hwang expands on the third feature by adding that "neutralisation arrangements come about as the result of great powers' agreement",[53] which means that a military stalemate is a necessary but not sufficient condition for neutralisation. An effective neutralisation also requires consensus and agreement among the neighbouring states and the great powers. David Martin, on the other hand, emphasises that for (armed) neutrality to work "a nation requires things: a united will, a territory strategically defensible and adequate human and material resources".[54]

While geography, capabilities, external competition, a situation of military stalemate, and a level of international acceptance are the main factors in making neutralisation a suitable policy, not all candidate states in the past have adopted a policy of permanent neutrality, and of those that did, few have been successful in sustaining and maintaining their permanent neutrality. This indicates that successful permanent neutrality has more nuances and conditions than those mentioned so far.

Neuhold has further expanded on neutrality conditions. He argued that there are at least five prerequisites for viable permanent neutrality, including:

1. Existence of a durable balance of power between/among the rival powers surrounding the neutral or candidate state
2. Low and manageable level of hostilities between/among the rival powers
3. Limited strategic importance of the neutral state. No great power would be ready to obtain control of the neutral state at a high price
4. Challenging geography and high cost of conquering and controlling the neutral state
5. Domestic stability, cohesion, and public support for permanent neutrality

Based on the study of neutrals in the nineteenth and early twentieth centuries, Cronin has also suggested that in relation to permanent neutrality "successes had four characteristics:

1. A form of public legitimation (by the Church, or by agreement from more than one power);
2. Challenging geographical features (which make a state hard to conquer and occupy);
3. Limited intrinsic strategic importance (not worth the sacrifice); and
4. Yet some economic value to the major powers (worth the agreement)".[55]

While Martin and Neuhold have included domestic factors as part of their suggested prerequisites for success, Cronin has focused only on the external ingredients of viable permanent neutrality.

The aforementioned sets of factors and variables for a viable and successful permanent neutrality could be classified under two broad categories:

1. External determinants, such as geopolitical position, the nature and scope of external powers' competition and hostilities, the dynamics

of international politics, and agreement of neighbouring states and the great powers

2. Internal determinants, such as internal stability, national cohesion, capability and public support for permanent neutrality

This brief literature review leads us to the conclusion that neutrality is a multi-dimensional concept, and one has to borrow insights from different approaches in IR to build a reasonably inclusive theoretical framework for the explanation of neutrality. Therefore, one cannot rely on a single IR theory while studying neutrality, as none of the theoretical approaches offer a comprehensive insight into the concept, evolution, and persistence of neutrality. While neo-realism is better at explaining neutrality as a foreign policy of small and weak states caught in geographical buffer zones, a constructivist approach offers a superior argument for the sustainability of neutrality in the post-Cold War era. Islamic international law (Siyar) also recognises neutrality largely as a pragmatic policy option, which Muslim polities could adopt under certain circumstances.

Neutrality in practice

As a tool of statecraft, the history of the concept of neutrality goes back to the years of political wrangling among the city-states in Ancient Greece, and the encounter between the Athenians and Melos.

In its earlier usage, particularly prior to the advent of the territorial state, neutrality was often considered a negative and suspicious phenomenon, particularly when the medieval principle of just war was a well-established doctrine in international politics. For example, when George William, the elector of Brandenburg, appealed to remain neutral in the war between Gustavus Adolphus, the king of Sweden, and the Holy Roman Emperor in 1630, Adolphus reacted thus: "what kind of a thing is that? Neutrality—I don't understand it. It is nothing to me".[56] In another instance during the proclamation of the Thirty Years' War, Adolphus is quoted as stating, "I shall treat neutrality as equivalent to a declaration of war against me".[57] In the same vein, Niccolo Machiavelli, a master of realpolitik, considered neutrality as a low moral position, which a prince should avoid.[58]

However, the practice of neutrality as a virtuous, state-centric legal and political position is a relatively new phenomenon.[59] The Congress of Vienna in 1815 for the first time recognised neutrality as a "strategic policy" for states and granted neutral status to Switzerland.[60] Neutrality was later codified in the Hague Conventions of 1899 and 1907 as "the first embodiment of neutral rights and duties under positivist international law".[61] The cantons of Switzerland developed a tradition of neutrality following agreement on a perpetual peace treaty with France in 1516; neutrality as an official policy position was, for the first time, mentioned in the Federal Diet in 1674 in reference to the hostilities between France and the Netherlands.[62]

After a period of Swiss entanglement in the intra-European conflict, the Treaty of 1815 made Switzerland the first permanently neutral state in the heart of Europe. It is fair to argue that the recognition of Switzerland's policy of permanent neutrality, stipulated in the Treaty of Paris and signed by Austria, France, Great Britain, Prussia, and Russia (the major European powers of the time) on 20 March 1815, injected neutrality into international political discourse.

The unique feature of Swiss permanent neutrality is that unlike later cases, such as Belgium, Luxembourg, Austria and Laos, the country historically and unilaterally adopted the status of neutrality, and it was unconditionally supported by the then great powers.[63]

In the cases of Belgium (1839) and Luxembourg (1867), neutralisation was imposed as a condition for granting and upholding the independence of the two small states, which were previously under the control of the Netherlands. Neutralisation of Belgium and Luxembourg was in large part a joint British and German design to contain France's regional ambitions. Hence, neutralisation and the limits it placed on the sovereignty of Belgium and Luxembourg were viewed by both nations as unjust. Belgium's neutrality came to a tragic end after the country was invaded by Germany in August 1914, with her status of permanent neutrality abolished in the Treaty of Versailles in 1919.[64] Luxembourg was also invaded by Germany during the First World War but did not abandon her neutrality until the end of the Second World War.

The permanent neutrality of Austria on the other hand was a compromise solution reached after a series of negotiations between the four occupation powers—France, the United Kingdom, the United States, and the USSR—and the Austrian government in the 1950s to end the country's occupation and return its full sovereignty. It paved the way for the signing of the Austrian State Treaty by the representatives of the occupation powers on 15 May 1955, and for the withdrawal of occupation forces.[65] Though the Austrian State Treaty declares that it has opted for permanent neutrality "on its own free will", Black argues that "[Austria] could only choose between continued occupation and permanent neutrality; it did not have the option of an independent foreign policy without obligations".[66]

The last and more complicated example of permanent neutrality was the neutralisation of Laos in 1962, as it was the first time a policy of permanent neutrality was applied outside Europe and in a situation where the number of stakeholders was larger and more diverse than in previous cases. Despite all the challenges, on 23 July 1962, the Kingdom of Laos and 14 regional and international parties signed the Declaration of Neutrality of Laos.[67] The signatories pledged to respect Laotian independence and refrain from intervening in the internal affairs of the country. The Declaration also placed certain conditions on the government of Laos regarding its foreign and security policy, which will be explained in detail in Chapter 3. The Laotian permanent neutrality, though not a very successful example, was a worthwhile endeavour aimed at reducing tensions in Southeast Asia, offering a negotiated settlement to domestic and regional problems facing Laos at the time.

In the categories of neutrals and un-aligned countries, there are many examples of the varying degrees of neutrality, mostly unilateral and unsanctioned. This type of neutrality has been practised in a number of small European states, such as Sweden, Finland, and the Republic of Ireland. Sweden opted for a policy of military neutrality in 1814, which makes it the oldest neutral country; despite having flexible foreign policy options in the post-war period it chose to remain neutral for many years. Sweden, even though not a permanently neutral state, adhered to both political and legal principles of neutrality.[68] In the cases of Finland and Ireland, given their geography, resources, and the dynamics of their relations with their big neighbours, sticking to a policy of neutrality seemed like a *sine qua non* as both countries had limited foreign policy options. However, some studies[69] do not agree with this notion and argue that the idea of neutrality, more than being a predicament, was a choice grounded in the domestic and ideational aspiration of these nations.[70]

Where the evolution and practice of neutrality in the 120-plus members of the Non-aligned Movement (NAM) is concerned, it is hard to find attributes of neutrality in the member states' pattern of behaviour that could conform to the duties, responsibilities, and norms upheld by traditional neutrals. Since the non-aligned countries defined their version of neutrality in relation to the Cold War power struggle, in the post-Cold War era their relevance as a group has substantially reduced. Perhaps the two features that still distinguish non-aligned countries from the rest are a refusal of membership to military alliances and active roles in UN peacekeeping missions.

Afghanistan was a founding member of the NAM, and for a long period non-alignment and impartial judgement were the traditional bases of its foreign policy.[71] However, Afghanistan's status as a non-aligned nation neither guaranteed peace nor prevented foreign occupation and interference in the country.

Notes

1   *OxfordDictionariesOnline*. Available at: http://oxforddictionaries.com/defin ition/english/neutrality.

2 Hague Convention (V) Respecting the Rights and Duties of Neutral Powers and Persons in Case of War on Land.
3 John Bouvier, *A Law Dictionary: Adapted to the Constitution and Laws of the United States of America, and of the Several States of the American Union: With References to the Civil and Other Systems of Foreign Law* (Philadelphia, PA: T. & J. W. Johnson, 1843), p. 772.
4 T. J. Lawrence, *War and Neutrality in the Far East* (London: Macmillan, 1904).
5 According to Agius and Devine, there is a lot of confusion over the terminology and labels used to denote this particular foreign and security policy (neutrality). See Christine Agius and Karen Devine, "Neutrality: A Really Dead Concept? A Reprise", *Cooperation and Conflict*, 46(3) (2011): 273.
6 Heiner Hanggi, "ASEAN and the ZOPFAN Concept", Regional Strategic Studies Programme, Institute of Southeast Asian Studies Singapore (1991), p. 3.
7 Cronin, "Thinking Long on Afghanistan", p. 56.
8 Black et al., *Neutralization and World Politics*, p. xi.
9 Peter Lyon, "Neutrality and Emergence of the Concept of Neutralism", *The Review of Politics*, 22(2) (April 1960): 267.
10 Agius, *The Social Construction of Swedish Neutrality*, p. 3.
11 In a more comprehensive manner, international relations (IR), "is a branch of political science" http://aiu.edu/publications.
12 Robert A. Bauslaugh, *The Concept of Neutrality in Classical Greece* (Berkeley, CA: University of California Press, 1991).
13 Agius and Devine, "Neutrality: A Really Dead Concept? A Reprise", pp. 265–284.
14 Jan Martin Rolence, "The Relevance of Neutrality in Contemporary International Relations", *Faculty of International Relations Working Papers* (University of Prague, 2008), p. 12.
15 Kenneth Waltz, *Theory of International Politics* (Boston, MA: Addison-Wesley, 1979), p. 97.
16 Michael F. Altfeld and Bruce Bueno de Mesquita, "Choosing Sides in War", *International Studies Quarterly*, 23(1) (1979): 87–112.
17 Agius contends that realists made neutrality fit their theory by emphasising that neutral states were following their own state-centred interests. See Agius, *The Social Construction of Swedish Neutrality*, pp. 36–37 and Jesse, "Choosing to Go It Alone: Irish Neutrality in Theoretical and Comparative Perspective", p. 1.
18 Rolence, "The Relevance of Neutrality in Contemporary International Relations", p. 12.
19 See Efraim Karsh, "International Co-operation and Neutrality", *Journal of Peace Research*, 25(1) (March 1988): 57–67, and Laurent Goetschel, "Neutrality, a Really Dead Concept?".
20 Jesse, "Choosing to Go It Alone: Irish Neutrality in Theoretical and Comparative Perspective", pp. 7–28.
21 Karen Devine, "Stretching the IR Theoretical Spectrum on Irish Neutrality: A Critical Social Constructivist Framework", *International Political Science Review*, 29 (4) (September 2008): 461.
22 Agius, *The Social Construction of Swedish Neutrality*, p. 4.
23 Karen Devine, 2008, "A Comparative Critique of the Practice of Irish Neutrality in the 'Unneutral' Discourse", *Irish Studies in International Affairs*, 19 (2008): 73–97.
24 Agius, *The Social Construction of Swedish Neutrality*, p. 45.

25 Goetschel, "Neutrality, a Really Dead Concept?" p. 116.
26 Ibid, 121.
27 Siyar is the plural form of the Arabic word *sirah* and means the method or way. Siyar denotes the method of the Muslims in their dealings with non-Muslims, enemy nations (*Ahl al-hrab*), contract partners (*Ahl al-a'hd*) as well as non-Muslim citizens (*Ahl al-dhimmah*), and temporary residents (*Musta'minun*). It is a branch of Islamic law (*fiqh*), based on the same sources and guided by the same maxims and principles as any other part of Shariáh. In contrast to public international law, it is therefore monistic.
28 Muhammad Hamidullah, *Muslim Conduct of State*, 1992, chapter 4 is dedicated to neutrality.
29 Majid Khadduri in his book *War and Peace in the Law of Islam* discusses neutrality.
30 Muhammad Abu Zahra, "International relation in Islam", *The First Conference of Academy of Islamic Research*, Cairo, 1968.
31 Zuḥaylī, Wahbah, *Athar al-Harb: fi al-Fiqh al-Islami* (Beirut: Dar al-Fikr, 1998) in Arabic.
32 Anke Iman Bouzenita, "The Principle of Neutrality and 'Islamic International Law' (Siyar)", *Global Jurist*, 11(1) (March 2011): Article 4.
33 Md. Akhir Hj. Yaacob, "The Law of Neutrality. A Comparative Study of Islamic Law and Public International Law" (PhD, University of Malaya, 1984). This is also considered major research on neutrality in Islam.
34 Karsh, *Neutrality and Small States*, pp. 1–2.
35 David S. Brackett, "International Relations à La Carte: A New Swiss Neutrality in Europe," *Weather Head Centre for International Affairs, Harvard University, WCFIA Working Paper 4* (1997), p. 2.
36 Muhammad Hamidullah, *The Muslim Conduct of State*, p. 301.
37 Majid Khadduri, *War and Peace in the Law of Islam* (New Jersey: The Lawbook Exchange, 2007), p. 251.
38 Verse 29 of Chapter 9 (Surat Al-Taubah), reads: "Fight those who do not believe in Allah or in the Last Day and who do not consider unlawful what Allah and His Messenger have made unlawful and who do not adopt the religion of truth from those who were given the Scripture—[fight] until they give the jizyah willingly while they are humbled".
39 Muhammad Haniff Hassan, "War, Peace or Neutrality: An Overview of Islamic Polity's Basis of Inter-State Relations", Rajaratnam School of International Studies (RSIS), 2007.
40 Verse 90 of Chapter 4 reads: "Except for those who take refuge with a people between yourselves and whom is a treaty or those who come to you, their hearts strained at [the prospect of] fighting you or fighting their own people. And if Allah had willed, He could have given them power over you, and they would have fought you. So if they remove themselves from you and do not fight you and offer you peace, then Allah has not made for you a cause [for fighting] against them".
41 Bouzenita, "The Principle of Neutrality and 'Islamic International Law' (Siyar)", p. 12.
42 Zuhayli's *Athar al-harb*. Quoted in Bouzenita, "The Principle of Neutrality and 'Islamic International Law'", p. 13.
43 In the very first centuries of Islam, non-Muslim Nubia (Sudan) and Abyssinia (Ethiopia) enjoyed a friendly status with the Islamic Empire and were considered

neutral states. See Khaled Abou El Fadal, *The Great Theft: Wrestling Islam from the Extremists* (New York, NY: Harper Collins Publishers, 2005), pp. 227–228.

44   Verse 74, Chapter 4, Surat Al-Taubah, *The Holy Qur'an* (The University of Leeds: Qurany Tool). Available at: http://comp.leeds.ac.uk/nora/html/9-74.html.

45   According to Ibn Kathir and Maududi the simple definition of hypocrites is "people who pretend to be Muslims in order to undermine Islam from within". See http://www.islam-watch.org/home/165-jon-mc/1504-hypocrites-according-to-the-koran.html.

46   Karsh, *Neutrality and Small States*, p. 1.

47   In this context *da'wah* is the function of the Caliph, extending authority over Muslims outside Islamic lands and promoting Islamic unity. In the twentieth century, *da'wah* has become the foundation for social, economic, political, and cultural activities. See http://oxfordislamicstudies.com/article/opr/t125/e511.

48   Bouzenita, "The Principle of Neutrality and 'Islamic International Law' (Siyar)", p. 20.

49   For details of modern Islamic scholars' views on neutrality, see Hassan, *War, Peace or Neutrality*, and Bouzenita, "The Principle of Neutrality and 'Islamic International Law' (Siyar)".

50   Black et al., *Neutralization and World Politics*, p. 67.

51   Karsh, *Neutrality and Small States*, p. 27.

52   Black et al., *Neutralization and World Politics*, p. 66.

53   In K. Hwang, *The Neutralized Unification of Korea in Perspective* (Cambridge, MA: Schenkman Pub. Co., 1980), p. 11.

54   David Martin, Philip Hind, and Vernon Huges, "Armed Neutrality for Australia". *Armed Neutrality Review*, 1 (April 1988): 1.

55   Cronin, "Thinking Long on Afghanistan", p. 58.

56   Sir Geoffrey Butler and S. Maccoby, *The Development of International Law* (London: Longmans, Green & Co., 1928), and Peter Lyon, "Neutrality and the Emergence of the Concept of Neutralism", *Review of Politics*, 22(2) (April 1960): 255–268.

57   David Evans, *Sherman's Horsemen: Union Cavalry Operations in the Atlanta Campaign* (Bloomington, IN: Indian University Press, 1999), p. 1.

58   Niccolo Machiavelli, *The Prince*. Translated by W. K. Marriot (London: J.M. Dent, 1958), p. 107. Available at: http://constitution.org/mac/prince.pdf.

59   C. G. Dehn, "Transactions of the Grotius Society", *Problems of Public and Private International Law, Transactions for the Year 1945* (Cambridge University Press), pp. 139–149. Retrieved from http://jstor.org/stable/743275.

60   The Congress of Vienna in 1815 announced Switzerland as a permanently neutral country and with this neutrality was for the first time accepted as a strategic policy of a state.

61   Christine Agius, *The Social Construction of Swedish Neutrality: Challenges to Swedish Identity and Sovereignty* (Manchester: Manchester University Press, 2006), 5.

62   Black et al., *Neutralization and World Politics*, p. 25.

63   Walther Hofer, *Neutrality as the Principle of Swiss Foreign Policy*. Translated by Mary Hottinger (Switzerland Spiegel Verlag, Zürich, 1957), p. 11.

64   Black et al., *Neutralization and World Politics*, p. 25.

65   Until 1955 the Soviet Union, Great Britain, United States, and France controlled different parts of Austria.

66   Black et al., *Neutralization and World Politics*, p. 29.

67 Burma, Cambodia, Canada, the People's Republic of China, the Democratic Republic of Vietnam, France, India, Poland, the Republic of Vietnam, Thailand, the Soviet Union, the United Kingdom, and the United States signed the declaration of neutralization of Laos.
68 Sweden eased its policy of strict neutrality after joining the EU in 1995.
69 Neal G. Jesse. "Choosing To Go It Alone: Irish Neutrality in Theoretical and Comparative Perspective", *International Political Science Review*, 27(1) (January 2006): 7–28.
70 Fred Singleton, "The Myth of 'Finlandisation'", *International Affairs*, 57(2) (Spring, 1981): 270–285.
71 Mohammad Khalid Ma'roof. *Afghanistan in World Politics: A Study in Afghan-US Relations* (New Delhi: Gian Publishing House, 1987), p. 9.

2 A framework for analysis

The following analytical framework is established to examine the viability and success of permanent neutrality. Neutrality variables presented below are derived from discussions on functions of neutralisation and the review of theoretical approaches in Chapter 1. For ease of analysis, these factors are placed in two categories: external factors/variables and internal factors/variables.

External factors/variables

Geopolitical position and importance

The term *geopolitics* denotes the relationship between geography and political and strategic decision making. According to *Merriam-Webster*, geopolitics is "a study of the influence of such factors as geography, economics, and demography on the politics, and especially the foreign policy, of a state".[1] As a distinct field of study, geopolitics was introduced by Halford Mackinder (1861–1947). In his famous article "The Geographical Pivot of History",[2] Mackinder presented a historical analysis of the connection between geography and socio-political developments in the world; however, the Swedish/German scholar Rudolf Kjellen coined the term *geopolitics* in 1899. Subsequently, German scholars such as Kjellen, Friedrich Ratzel,[3] and Karl Haushofer[4] rigorously studied the influences of geographic and demographic factors on power relationships in continental Europe and excelled in the field of geopolitics. In its contemporary usage, however, geopolitics is often a military and strategic concept focused on analysing the significance of areas of land, sea, and space based on the perceived interest of the great powers.

Geopolitical position on the other hand refers to the economic and strategic relevance of a state's location in the context of regional and international power politics. Geopolitical significance, or lack of it, depends on the special economic and geographical features of a state in relation to its neighbouring and global powers. States that are located adjacent to major natural resources, communication and transit routes, straits, and sea lines, or in a zone of competitive interest of two or more great powers are considered strategically vital. The great powers either are in control of such strategically vital areas or are determined to exercise control, even if it comes with a price. Hence, strategically vital states are not suitable candidates for permanent neutrality. According to Neuhold, "[A neutral's] territory must not be regarded as so vitally important by any Great Powers that it would be ready to pay even higher prices to obtain the possession of that piece of land".[5] States with significant but not vital geopolitical features could find permanent neutrality a practical foreign policy.

Geopolitical position therefore is an important determinant of whether a state could choose a policy of permanent neutrality or not. Karsh argues that "action and interaction of states, as well as friendships and enmities among them, are determined largely by geo-strategic realities".[6] In the case of small and weaker states located in a zone of great powers contestation, geopolitical features, most importantly their geography and the nature of contestation among the surrounding powers, act as a kind of force majeure that leaves the small and strategically located states with limited foreign and security policy options.

Dynamics of external powers' conflict and competition (balance of power)

Study of conflicts and their dynamics requires an extensive and multidisciplinary approach, which is beyond the scope of this section. However, to facilitate their understanding and examination, scholars of IR have attempted to categorise conflicts into different stages. Alker, Gurr, and Rupesinghe,[7] for example, have categorised conflicts, on the basis of three main variables: *use of violence*, *level of groups' hostilities*, and *sequential expectations*, into the following six phases:

1. Dispute/conflict emergence
2. Crisis/escalation
3. Limited violence
4. Massive violence
5. Abatement/de-escalation
6. Settlement

Each stage of conflict demands a different conflict management strategy. Neutralisation, according to Black, could be applied in two periods within the cycle of conflict. The first period takes place between stages two and three mentioned above, which are moving from crisis into limited violence. The goal of neutralisation in this period would be to "prevent the outbreak of a violent clash in an area already subject to the intrusion of competitive political interests of outside actors".[8] The second period, at stage five, is abatement or military stalemate "in which neither side can hope to gain a decisive advantage at the existing level of conflict and in which the principal parties fear the consequences of uncontrolled escalation".[9] The goal at the military stalemate stage would be to terminate or at least moderate the conflict.

Neuhold, on the other hand, exclusively stresses the military stalemate phase featuring a balance of power and conflict abatement or *détente*, as the key conditions for a successful neutralisation. He argues that "an approximate balance of power between adversaries in whose conflict a neutral wish not to be involved" and "low conflict intensity between conflicting parties"[10] are equally important prerequisites for viable permanent neutrality. Edgar Bonjour has also underlined the need for a balance between conflict parties, arguing that "equilibrium of rival great powers is the air in which neutrality of small states thrives".[11]

Consensus and agreement of neighbouring and the great powers

The word *consensus* is derived from the Latin root *consentire*, which means: "to feel the same"; however, a more refined definition of consensus is "an idea or opinion that is shared by all the people in a group".[12] In the field of conflict management, where it is mostly used, consensus is defined as a cooperative group process where all group members see the final outcome as agreeable. According to Butler and Rothstein, "consensus strives to take into account everyone's concerns and resolve them before any decision is made".[13] However, it has been emphasised that consensus is not unanimity, and the final outcome of the process will not be the best preference of each participant.

Building consensus among the stakeholders in conflicts is one of the key steps before an agreement is reached. In situations of regional and international conflict, a military stalemate is often seen as a prelude to crafting consensus on alternative (non-military) solutions, such as neutralisation. Thus, antagonists could consider neutralisation as a consensus resolution to their dispute.

In the case of neutralisation, a consensus may emerge among the major stakeholders that declaring the state in question permanently neutral will serve everyone's relative interest. Such consensus is normally followed by a neutralisation agreement, which is either drafted and signed or endorsed and guaranteed by regional and international stakeholders. Existence of a multilateral agreement is a major condition that distinguishes permanent neutrality from other forms of neutrality. According to Wicker:

> permanent neutrality exists by reason of treaties alone and has no other authority than that conferred in their provision. No state can neutralise itself, however faithfully at whatever cost the principle of neutralisation may be observed. A contract and the interdependent relationship of several states is in all cases necessary.[14]

International recognition, in the form of an agreement or treaty among the external powers to uphold, respect, and, in some instances, guarantee the sovereignty of the candidate state, has been an integral feature of all previous instances of neutralisation.

Internal factors

Stability and cohesion

It is worth remembering that the basic premise of our analysis of viability, with regard to permanent neutrality, is that the subjects of neutralisation are sovereign states; hence, domestic stability is the most important prerequisite for any policy to be successfully implemented within a state. Domestic stability and cohesion are more a condition than a concept. Achieving it requires certain minimal criteria of governance, such as legitimacy, maintenance of law and order, provision of public services, and social solidarity and unity.[15] The simplest definition of domestic stability is: "the absence of large-scale violence within a country".[16] More precisely, adding the word "continuing" before "large scale violence" denotes and underlines the minimum condition needed for maintenance of neutrality. The prevalence of large-scale domestic violence weakens state authority and erodes public trust, national cohesion, and a sense of belonging and citizenship. Neuhold has stressed domestic stability and cohesion as an important condition for upholding and maintaining neutrality, arguing that "domestic instability in a neutral state could tempt others to fish in troubled political waters there".[17] Prolonged domestic instability can also lead to cross-border violence, infiltration, and subversion by neighbouring states, which further exacerbates the challenges of maintaining a policy of permanent neutrality. According to Black, "when a neutralized state is vulnerable to other forms of interventionist coercion and perhaps already subject to such intervention, redoubtable problems of control and enforcement are apt to arise".[18] Hence, successful neutralisation largely depends on domestic stability and cohesion of the subject states.

Military and economic capabilities

Military and economic capabilities form the key bases of a nation's power. The military capability of a nation is directly connected to its financial, physical, and technological resources, which are collectively referred to as economic capabilities. A state's economic capability or power is "the capacity to influence other states through economic means. It is composed of a country's industrial base, natural resources, capital, technology, geographic position, health system and education system".[19]

It is argued that for a state to function properly, it has to possess at least four basic capacities: (1) extractive capacity; (2) steering capacity; (3) legitimation capacity; and (4) coercive capacity.[20] However, in the current analysis of the viability of neutralisation, we are not concerned with properly functioning states, as the candidates for permanent neutrality are often weak and small states and neutralisation is proposed as the least unsatisfactory choice when seeking to end external intervention and provide space for socio-economic development. According to Josef Kunz, it is the duty of a neutral state to "have an adequate army, to have fortifications and to make all necessary military preparations in order to be able to defend itself ... best guarantee of permanent neutrality is a strong army and the unshakeable determination to defend this neutrality against any comer, as history has proved in the model case of Switzerland".[21] Acknowledging this point, we, however, opt to take a modest principle suggested by Neuhold in regard to a neutral state's capacity, which is that neutrals should be able to make an aggressor pay more than a token "entrance and occupation price".[22] The threshold of a neutral or candidate's state capabilities, therefore, could be limited to a level of military and economic power sufficient to deny the possible aggressor state an outright military victory and prevent it from achieving its political objectives. Neutral or candidate states' economic capacity should cover basic security and public services from their own resources, with the state not being overly dependent on financial and material support from any one of the conflicting states or a great power with political and strategic agendas inside the state itself.

Together, the above-mentioned external and internal factors provide an analytical framework, presented in Table 2.1, for studying the viability and sustainability of permanent neutrality.

Summary

The chapter presented a theoretical framework, arguing that a combination of external factors, such as a state's geopolitical position, the nature of external powers' conflict, and consensus and formal agreement among external powers on neutralisation of the candidate country, are the key determinants

Table 2.1 A proposed analytical framework of viability and sustainability of permanent neutrality

External factor + Internal factors = Viable permanent neutrality

External factors/Determinants	Internal factors/Determinants
1. Appropriate geopolitical position and importance	4. Domestic stability and cohesion
2. Appropriate external conditions, balance of power, and military stalemate	5. Capabilities, military and economic
3. Consensus and agreement of neighbouring and the great powers	

of viable and sustainable permanent neutrality. While previous studies of neutrality have focused on external determinants as the main elements of neutralisation, the current theoretical framework has also incorporated two internal factors, believed to be vital in making permanent neutrality work. Domestic stability/cohesion and military and economic capacity of candidate states are among the chief internal determinants of successful neutralisation. It has been acknowledged that the present analytical framework, anchored on five external and internal factors, is in no way a comprehensive structure for studying a complex phenomenon such as neutrality. In the following chapters, we will use this framework as an instrument to analyse the success and failure of permanent neutrality in Switzerland, Austria, and Laos as well as the feasibility and desirability of Afghanistan's permanent neutrality.

Notes

1 "Geopolitics", *Merriam-Webster* dictionary online, 8 July 2014. Available at: http://merriam-webster.com/dictionary/geopolitics.
2 Halford J. Mackinder, "The Geographical Pivot of History," *The Geographical Journal*, 23(4) (1904): 421–437.
3 Friedrich Ratzel, "Studies in Political Areas: The Political Territory in Relation to Earth and Continent", *The American Journal of Sociology*, 3(3) (November 1897): 297–313.
4 Karl Haushofer, "Why Geopolitik?" eds. Gerard Toal, Simon Dalby, and Paul Routledge, *The Geopolitics Reader* (London: Routledge, 1998), pp. 33–36.
5 Neuhold, "The Neutral States of Europe", p. 132.
6 Karsh, *Neutrality and Small States*, p. 81.
7 H. R. Alker, T. R. Gurr, and K. Rupesinghe. *Journeys through Conflict Narratives and Lessons* (Rowman & Littlefield, 2001), p. 336.
8 Black et al., *Neutralization and World Politics*, p. 67.
9 Ibid, p. 67.
10 Neuhold, "The Neutral States of Europe", p. 132.
11 Edgar Bonjour, *Swiss Neutrality: Its History and Meaning*, Translated by M. Hottinger (London: George Allen & Unwin London, 1946).

12 http://merriam-webster.com/dictionary/consensus.
13 C. T. Butler and A. Rothstein, "On Conflict and Consensus", *A Hand Book of Formal Consensus Decision Making*. Accessed on 12 July 2014. Available at: www.consensus.net/pdf/consensus.pdf.
14 Cyrus French Wicker, *Neutralization* (London: Oxford University Press, 1911), p. 2.
15 See Nayef R. F. Al-Rodhan and Sara Kuepfer, *Stability of States: Nexus between Transnational Threats, Globalization, and Internal Resilience* (Genève: Slatkine Edition, 2007).
16 Laurie Nathan, "Security Communities and the Problem of Domestic Instability", *Crisis States Program, Working Series Paper No.1*. Available at: eprints.lse.ac.uk/28204/1/wp55.
17 Neuhold, "The Neutral States of Europe", p. 133.
18 Black et al., *Neutralization and World Politics*, p. xvii.
19 James Graham, "Military Power vs Economic Power in History", *HistoryOrb.com*. (2014). Available at: http://historyorb.com/world/power.php.
20 The four basic state capacities are (1) the capacity to mobilise financial resources from the society to pursue what the central policymakers perceive as the "national interest" (extractive capacity); (2) the capacity to guide national socio-economic development (steering capacity); (3) the capacity to dominate by using symbols and creating consensus (legitimation capacity); and (4) the capacity to dominate by the use or threat of force (coercive capacity). See Andrew G. Walder ed., *The Waning of the Communist State: Economic Origins of Political Decline in China and Hungary* (Berkeley, CA: University of California Press, 1995).
21 Josef L. Kunz, "Austria's Permanent Neutrality, Reviewed Work", *The American Journal of International Law*, 50(2) (April 1956): 418.
22 Neuhold, "The Neutral States of Europe", p. 132.

3 Prominent cases of permanent neutrality—Switzerland, Austria, and Laos

This chapter briefly examines the development of the policy of permanent neutrality in Switzerland, Austria, and Laos. While these three cases share certain common features—such as difficult terrain, no direct access to the sea, and being surrounded by powerful and hostile neighbours—the context, motivation, trajectory, and outcomes of their policies of neutrality substantially differ from each other. Switzerland is the oldest neutral country and the only one whose permanent neutrality survived for nearly two hundred years and through the two World Wars. By contrast, Austria and Laos were made permanently neutral in the second half of the twentieth century. Swiss permanent neutrality was a product of the post-Napoleonic balance of the power system in Europe; however, permanent neutrality of Austria and Laos was seen as an instrument of conflict management aimed at the reduction of hostilities between Cold War rival blocs.

Each case study is divided into two parts. The first part presents a brief introduction to the development of the policy of permanent neutrality, and the second part examines the presence and impact of the five factors of the analytical framework, namely: (1) geopolitical position and importance, (2) balance of power, (3) consensus and agreement among neighbouring and the great powers, (4) domestic stability and cohesion, and (5) military and economic capabilities.

Permanent neutrality of Switzerland

Officially, at least since the 1815 Congress of Vienna, neutrality has become an inseparable characteristic of Switzerland's history and identity. Today, the notion of Swiss neutrality is principally coterminous with the idea of a Swiss nation. However, this often-revered Swiss tradition of neutrality evolved through decades of proxy wars, internal conflict, and continuous existential threats posed by its powerful neighbours, such as imperial France, Germany, and Austria. According to Kate Morris and Timothy

White, "historically, the Swiss policy of neutrality can best be understood as a reaction against the real and threatened domination from other larger more powerful states, especially its neighbours".[1]

The evolution of Swiss neutrality

While it is difficult to locate a certain point in history as the time of its inception, the idea of neutrality emerged in the discourse among the cantons of Swiss Confederation after it suffered a heavy defeat at the Battle of Marignano in 1515. According to historian William Denison McCracken, the defeat at the hands of a superior and better-organised French army in the plains of northern Italy was a point of departure for new and more pragmatic practices of governance and foreign relations in the Confederation. After this battle, the Swiss recognised that they "no longer were able to decide European issues by the weight of their influence."[2] Swiss leaders quickly realised that engaging in European power politics demanded at the very least a unified defence and foreign policy strategy, which in turn required inter-state cohesion and establishment of a central authority akin to those of the neighbouring states, such as France and Germany. In a loose Confederation composed of various religious, ethnic, and linguistic groups, such an undertaking was certainly unfeasible. Moreover, the concept of centralisation was in contradiction with the spirit of individual freedom and cantonal autonomy, which were the fundamental principles of the Swiss system of governance. As a result, the Confederation decided to restrain its practice of wild militarism and foreign adventurism and instead embrace a policy of "sitting still" or keeping aloof from conflicts among regional powers while staying prepared to defend its territory when attacked. The idea of Swiss neutrality therefore has a pragmatic character rooted in safeguarding Switzerland's sovereignty and autonomy by taking all necessary measures to avoid entanglement in others' conflict.

The early period: Self-declared neutrality

The Confederation applied a whole range of state resources—diplomatic, political, military, and economic—to defend and promote its neutrality. At the diplomatic level, while there were no international legal mechanisms during this period to regulate and guarantee the state's neutrality, the Swiss developed a system of bilateral treaties with the neighbouring powers to institutionalise and reinforce their policy of neutrality. The earliest examples of institutionalisation of neutrality, according to Edgar Bonjour, were the signing of "the perpetual peace with Francis I of 1516 and the protective alliance of 1521. In these two treaties, the Confederation committed itself to never permitting its soldiery to be used against the King of France and to close the Alpine passes to his enemies".[3] Occasionally these treaties, including the Eternal Pact, which the Confederation signed with her archenemy Austria in 1511, contradicted each other. However, as part of the development of its neutrality, the Swiss quickly learnt how to reconcile these contradictions and navigate their way through inconsistencies in their commitments and promises. The Confederation cleverly used its strategic assets, such as control of the alpine passes and the services of fearless soldiers, in different combinations to secure long-time peace treaties with her powerful neighbours and to maintain the balance of power in the region.

At the domestic political level, adoption of neutrality as a state policy and the necessity of joint national defence demanded increased coordination and cooperation among different cantons and strengthening federal institutions. In this period, nine adjacent small states and territories joined the Confederation, raising the total number of cantons to 22 from its earlier 13. This fairly voluntary expansion moulded the Swiss Confederation into a solid geographical unit with defined and mostly defendable frontiers.

The era of Reformation and Counter-Reformation resulted in the Thirty Years' War, which exacerbated religious, ethnic, and political cleavages between the Protestant and Catholic parts of Switzerland, and disrupted the nascent process of formation of a national authority. However, despite attempts by certain Catholic and Protestant groups to push the country to engage in Europe's religious war, Bonjour argues that "the Confederation eluded the danger by girding on the armour of neutrality; it did not completely cut Switzerland off from the outside world, but protected her from military embroilment".[4] The 1648 Peace of Westphalia formally recognised the Confederation's territorial integrity and independence, and a neutral Switzerland emerged, which was stronger and more cohesive as a nation than ever before.

Cognisant of the realities of the European power struggle, the cantons, Catholic and Protestant, finally decided to contribute to the formation of federal forces and adoption of a defensive doctrine called Federal Bastions. A major element of the Federal Bastion strategy, according to Bonjour, was the creation of "a belt of neutralized zones, in which all military actions should be prohibited,"[5] to protect Switzerland from coming into direct contact with the surrounding conflicting parties.[6]

This indicated the Confederation's commitment to defend its neutrality. However, besides domestic measures, maintenance of neutrality was also a function of external factors, most importantly the dynamics of relations among the surrounding great powers. At the external level, manifestation of a balance of power in the early sixteenth century, with France and Austria (the houses of Hapsburg and Bourbon) as its main protagonists and Britain often acting as the balancer, enabled Switzerland to adopt and maintain neutrality. The Confederation at times helped this system of balance of power in Europe by equal treatment of its neighbouring powers. In all, as noted by Leo Schelbert, despite political and administrative inefficiencies and challenges, during the early phase of the Confederacy's rule from 1516 to 1799, Switzerland enjoyed relative peace and stability.[7] The rise of Napoleon Bonaparte (1799–1815) eventually disrupted this long era of a balance of power, destabilised Europe, and brought an end to the first phase of Swiss neutrality.

The French invasion and disruption of neutrality

While carefully guarding its neutrality, Switzerland maintained a close and friendly relationship with its mighty neighbour, France, for over a century. This rather amicable arrangement came to a tragic end when in 1798 France invaded Switzerland and turned it into a satellite state. The French abolished the Confederation system, removed the Diet and in its place established a centralised Helvetic Republic with a two-tier legislative body: a Senate and a Grand Council. To consolidate its control further, after crushing pockets of armed resistance in the Schwiz, Uri, and Zug cantons, in August 1799, the French Government concluded a Treaty of Alliance with the newly established Helvetic Republic.[8] The political structure and military alliance of the Helvetic Republic defied centuries-old Swiss political traditions of cantonal autonomy and military neutrality and inevitably met with stiff public resistance. In the summer of 1802, people from all over the country revolted against the new order. Armed conflicts erupted in Zurich, Unterwalden, and Bern in which the Helvetic Republic forces were defeated.[9] While the Helvetic Republic was almost a lost cause, understanding the nature of Swiss politics, Napoleon saved France's right over Switzerland's affairs. In a famous Act of Mediation, he rather cunningly acknowledged the need to restore the federal system and respect Swiss neutrality. Speaking to a group of Swiss emissaries in Lausanne, Napoleon emphasised:

> the more I thought over the nature of your country, the stronger became my conviction that it was impossible to subject it to any uniform system on account of the diversity of its component parts; everything drives you to federalism … You need rest, independence and a neutrality acknowledged by all powers surrounding you.[10]

Napoleon restored certain features of the confederate system; however, in reality, Switzerland effectively remained a French dominion until the Congress of Vienna in 1815.

The French invasion and the disruption of the balance of power turned Switzerland into the battlefield of a bloody war between Napoleon's France and an alliance of Austria, Britain, and Russia, during which the Confederation strove to reassert its neutral position and pleaded with the warring nations, albeit in vain, to refrain from violating the country's neutrality. The most illustrious, yet disappointing, example of such an attempt was when Landamman Reinhard, the envoy of the Diet, pleaded with imperial France to respect Swiss neutrality during war against Austria in 1809, to which Napoleon arrogantly replied, *"Vis-à-vis de moi, cette neutralite est un mot vide de sens qui ne vous sert qu'autant que je le veux"*,[11] meaning that to me your neutrality is a word without meaning, which is useful to you only in as far as I want it. Hofer noted that this episode and later attempts by the strong men of Europe, such as Prince Metternich of Austria, Napoleon III, and Bismarck, to humiliate the Swiss and violate their neutrality, left an enduring scar on the political consciousness of the Swiss people.[12]

The new era Congress of Vienna and proclamation of permanent neutrality

After 15 years under French suzerainty and becoming the battlefield of a European power struggle, the Congress of Vienna in 1815 ended the Napoleonic era and redrew the map of Europe. The great powers eventually reached a consensus, as Bonjour argues, that "not [only] the neutrality, but also the integrity and sovereignty of Switzerland are in the true interest of Europe".[13] Henceforth, the five major powers at the congress, namely, Austria, France, Great Britain, Prussia, and Russia, formally declared Switzerland a permanently neutral state and offered to guarantee its neutrality and integrity.[14]

Affirmed and guaranteed by the regional powers, the 1815 Neutrality Act made Switzerland the first recognised permanently neutral state in history. Hofer claims that from this point onwards neutrality also "became an integral element of the European Law of Nations".[15] Jealously protected ever since, the concept of permanent neutrality grew into a fundamental part of Swiss identity. As a foreign and security policy option, Switzerland's permanent neutrality set a useful precedent that was later followed by a number of small European states.

This brief examination of Switzerland's neutrality during the two historical periods, 1516–1799 and 1799–1815, indicates that preservation of neutrality depended more than anything else on the existence of a balance of power in the surrounding region.

Except for occasional threats from neighbouring powers, such as the newly rising German state, Swiss permanent neutrality did not face a serious challenge from external sources for nearly a century after it was recognised by the Congress of Vienna; however, on the domestic front, the country endured remarkable upheavals. Religious cleavages and ethnic hostilities divided the Confederation into unionist and secessionist halves and culminated in a civil war in 1847–1848. While the war ended with a decisive victory for the unionist forces, a new constitution was drafted to meet the aspirations of both sides for a united Confederation but with diverse and autonomous cantons determined to protect and nurture the country's neutrality.

Notwithstanding religious and political rifts, the Swiss have always converged on preservation of their neutrality. The concept of neutrality has often functioned as a magical glue tying together diverse and fiercely independent cantons that hardly agreed on anything else; for example, during the Congress of Vienna, the Swiss delegation composed of both the old forces (the *conservatives*) and the new forces (the *liberals*) "stood in each other's way to make any meaningful and united progress impossible".[16] The delegates were fiercely at odds with each other on many issues, including demarcation of frontiers, cantonal constitutions, and division of authorities; as Bonjour notes, "at one point, however, all dissention, all inter-cantonal disputes were silenced—namely, the question of neutrality".[17] Neutrality also remained a matter of consensus at the domestic and inter-canton debates, such that, for its preservation, the cantons agreed once again to raise a confederate army and bring all foreign relations into the domain of the Diet, abolishing the mercenary system and prohibiting the receipt of outside military titles and pensions by Swiss citizens.

The Swiss recognised that their internal cohesion and economic opportunities were linked to the country's external neutrality. Bonjour further notes that "the Swiss man in the street began to regard neutrality as a protective rampart behind which he could go about his business in perfect security".[18]

On the other hand, the austere practice of political neutrality made Switzerland a favourable venue for mediation of conflicts and a trusted host for the first modern international organisations, such as the International Committee of the Red Cross, the Universal Postal Union, the International Labor Organization, and the League of Nations. While Switzerland's provision of "good offices" as noted by John F. L. Ross has "been another offshoot of permanent neutrality",[19] the reverse causality holds equally true. That is, services such as providing neutral meeting venues and hosting international organisations increased Switzerland's reputation as a neutral state and further strengthened its position among belligerent nations.

Consolidation of neutrality and its challenges in the twentieth century

Between the Congress of Vienna in 1815 and the eruption of the First World War in 1914, Europe witnessed its longest era of political stability, rapid industrialisation, and economic growth. This long period of stability also enabled Switzerland to consolidate its internal security and preserve and promote its neutrality. While Swiss neutrality faced its real test of endurance in the first half of the twentieth century, the Confederation had to take certain military and diplomatic actions during the otherwise peaceful nineteenth century to preserve its neutrality against external threats. For example, in 1870, when France and Germany, two of the guarantors of Swiss permanent neutrality, declared war on each other, Switzerland had little option but to prepare for self-defence. The Confederation mobilised five divisions of her armed forces totalling more than 37,000 soldiers, prohibited Swiss merce-naries from joining either side, and embargoed supply of lethal materials on the belligerents. With these brazen actions, Switzerland displayed the extent to which she was ready to go in order to protect her neutrality while both belligerent nations actively encouraged it to join their side in the war.[20] On another occasion, in 1889, Germany threatened to withdraw its guarantee of Switzerland's permanent neutrality when the Confederation provided asy-lum to German socialists and anarchists and expelled a German spy. This time, the Swiss ceded some ground to ensure the German guarantee of its neutrality by, for example, agreeing to limit the action of German refugees and signing new instruments of conflict settlements.

During the First and Second World Wars, Switzerland managed to avoid the devastation and despair that befell the rest of Europe, not only by vir-tue of its permanent neutrality but also due to a combination of other fac-tors, such as its formidable geography, economic utility and humanitarian service to the belligerent, agile and tough military forces, and above all, a healthy dose of luck. For instance, at the beginning of the First World War, the Confederation mobilised her entire armed force and reinforced her frontier defence posts in the north and west corners of the country border-ing France and Germany. While in the early days of war, Germany invaded Luxembourg and Belgium, two fellow neutral states, Bonjour underlines that "merciful fate spared the Swiss army the necessity of proving that it was equal to any attempt at a break-through by foreign troops".[21] Switzerland remained neutral and at the end of the war, the Great Powers once again reiterated their support for permanent neutrality of Switzerland as enshrined in Article 435 of the Treaty of Versailles.[22]

Likewise, during the Second World War, Switzerland made it clear that she was willing and ready to preserve and defend her neutrality by all means, including military. While according to McConnell, "during the Second World War both the Germans and the allies explicitly recognised the permanently neutral status of Switzerland in diplomatic notes",[23] a German invasion of Switzerland, particularly after the fall of France, appeared imminent. However, apart from a myriad of other factors, such as the high cost of invasion and occupation,[24] John Dreyer and Neal Jesse argue that the "Germans' campaign in the East against the Soviets played an enormous role in reducing the threat of invasion".[25] Notwithstanding certain critics of Switzerland's subtle connivance with Nazi Germany during the war,[26] the Confederation preserved her neutrality in accordance with the provision of international law, particularly the Hague Conventions of 1907. The country, at the same time, continued to provide a neutral venue for negotiation among the belligerents and a safe haven for the victims of war—a role which she played successfully during the Cold War, and which she continues to play even today.

Analysis of Swiss neutrality

While there is still debate among the scholars of IR whether Swiss neutrality is an exception or a model applicable to other countries, Switzerland is hailed as a rare case of success among a dozen or so nations that tried in vain to remain neutral. John Dreyer and Neal Jesse attribute the success of Swiss neutrality to three major factors: first, the incorporation of an armed deterrent into the national culture; second, the provision of neutrality as a collective good; and third, the solidification of Swiss neutrality in international law, custom, and convention for nearly 200 years.[27]

External factors

Geopolitical position and importance

The geopolitical location of Switzerland, a small rugged and landlocked Confederation surrounded by major European powers of the time, such as France, the Holy Roman Empire, and later, Germany, Austria, and Italy, has been a crucial factor in shaping her policy of neutrality. Switzerland's geographical position, according to McCracken, "imposes upon her the choice between two utterly distinct foreign policies. She must either cast in her lot with one of the rival European powers, or else she must observe strict neutrality toward them all".[28] The Confederation chose the latter, and beside other military and political factors, Hofer notes, "geographical factors, in particular the strategically important key position of the Alpine massif, have also contributed to the growth of Swiss neutrality".[29] The geographical position of Switzerland is therefore undoubtedly an important factor in Swiss neutrality; however, from a strategic point of view, it is equally plausible to argue that the difficult terrain and formidable communication and logistics challenges that such geography produces made the country less desirable for military actions and actual power projection by the great powers. This fact, in turn, reduced her strategic attractiveness and made it easier for Switzerland to remain neutral. Moreover, in some instances, notwithstanding challenges, militarily violations of Swiss neutrality may have looked appealing, but the invader would have run the risk of pushing Switzerland to siding with the enemy, which, given her strategic position, as such could have upset the balance of power.

The balance of power

Looking at the evolution of Swiss neutrality, it is evident that a balance of power has been a prominent factor in enabling Switzerland to maintain its neutrality, particularly between the mid-sixteenth and the early twentieth centuries.

Similarly, reinstatement of Swiss neutrality and its recognition during the 1815 Congress of Vienna was a direct consequence of an attempt by the great powers to restore and institutionalise a system of balance of power in Europe. Therefore, one can safely argue that Swiss neutrality, particularly during the nineteenth century, was a by-product of the post-1815 system of balance of power.

Consensus and agreement among neighbouring countries and the great powers

Switzerland proclaimed neutrality from the middle of the sixteenth century, yet her status was neither recognised nor respected by its neighbouring powers. Although it is difficult to say whether a formal agreement on Swiss neutrality would have deterred Napoleon from occupying Switzerland, in the absence of such an obligation, he called the self-declared Swiss neutrality a word without meaning. However, after the emergence of a consensus among external stakeholders on the need for Switzerland's neutrality, the organisers of the 1815 Congress of Vienna formally declared Switzerland a permanently neutral state and committed to guaranteeing its neutrality. An international agreement, such as the declaration of permanent neutrality of Switzerland, also creates legal and moral obligations under international law for signatories to respect and safeguard their commitment toward the neutral state. One can attribute the non-violation of Swiss neutrality during the First World War and its reiteration in the Treaty of Versailles in

1919 to a general consensus among the great powers on the usefulness of Switzerland's neutrality.

Domestic factors

Stability and cohesion

Switzerland occasionally underwent ethnic and religious conflicts and at one point in the mid-nineteenth century had a secessionist movement and a brief civil war. However, except during the 15 years under *de facto* French rule from 1799 to 1814, the Confederation did not experience continuous large-scale violence as detrimental to state authority, maintenance of law and order or the state's ability to uphold its commitments to neutrality. In contrast, one of the strongest features of Swiss neutrality was the overwhelming popular support for neutrality among the leadership of various cantons. While it is hard to gauge the impact of domestic stability and cohesion on the maintenance of Swiss permanent neutrality, the case study reveals that the concept and practice of neutrality had a profound impact on building domestic cohesion and enhancing the sense of solidarity among leaders of different cantons. According to Bonjour, when it came to neutrality all inter-cantonal disputes were silenced and instead a spirit of cooperation prevailed. Moreover, neutrality functioned as a uniting factor for an otherwise multi-ethnic and diverse group of people and was the main force that encouraged the Swiss to raise a federal army and build a modern state.

Military and economic capabilities

As highlighted in the above case study, Switzerland has pioneered the principle of armed neutrality. As early as the mid-seventeenth century, the Confederation adopted a defensive doctrine called Federal Bastions and relied on native resources to defend its neutrality. While the 1815 Act of Neutrality offered certain security assurances and created a moral obligation for signatories to respect Switzerland's neutrality, when faced with credible threat the Confederation did not merely rely on guarantees offered by the great powers but also mobilised all its available resources, including military, to protect its neutrality.

Switzerland demonstrated its military strength and determination to use force to safeguard its neutrality during the two World Wars. Even before the First World War Switzerland was one of the most industrialised countries in Europe. While accurate gross domestic product (GDP) per capita figures are available only after the 1950s, according to Maddison Historical GDP estimates, in 1914 Switzerland had a GDP per capita of US$4,233 and in

1940 this figure rose to US$6,397. At the outbreak of the Second World War, Switzerland was the second richest country in Europe after the United Kingdom.

The Swiss were perfectly willing to use economic strength to maintain a capable army; as Henry Steiger points out, "when in 1936 a loan of $53,500,000 for the reorganisation of the army was floated, it was oversubscribed 42 per cent. The money was used for increased training and new fortifications".[30] Historical facts and figures about Switzerland clearly indicate that its military and economic capabilities were above the minimum level identified by our analysis framework.

Summary

Switzerland is the birthplace of the policy of permanent neutrality where the idea of neutrality was successfully put into practice. After recognising the failure of the country's expansionist foreign military ventures and the cost of entanglement in the conflict of her powerful neighbours, the Confederation decided to stay away from others' conflicts as it didn't want to risk being absorbed by one of its more dominant neighbours.

Since the early sixteenth century, a mixture of domestic and trans-border factors, such as bilateral peace treaties and the Federal Bastions policy, on one hand, and formidable geography of the mountain nation and the persistence of a regional balance of power, on the other hand, enabled Switzerland to preserve her policy of neutrality for many centuries. The policy also enjoyed support at the canton level and served as a uniting factor for an otherwise multi-ethnic and diverse group of people. After a brief period of disruption during the Napoleonic era, the great powers officially recognised Switzerland as a permanently neutral state at the Congress of Vienna in 1815, and its status was reconfirmed in the Treaty of Versailles in 1919. Switzerland employed all its military, economic, and political resources, and provided humanitarian services and meeting spaces during major conflicts and wars to protect and promote its neutrality.

The case study of Austria

Austria's trajectory toward permanent neutrality was quite different in purpose and process from that of Switzerland. In Switzerland, neutrality at various points of time functioned as an instrument for terminating, managing, and preventing conflicts; however, in the case of Austria, permanent neutrality mainly served as a tool for conflict avoidance and restoration of Austrian sovereignty. Similarly, in terms of its development, Swiss permanent neutrality evolved through decades of practice, failure, and adaptation, while Austrian permanent neutrality was the outcome of a series of negotiations between 1947 and 1955, between Austria and the major stakeholders, mainly the Soviet Union and the United States, but also Britain and France. The negotiations were aimed at establishing a free, independent, and sovereign Austria based on the 1943 Moscow Joint Four Nations Declaration.[31]

While the two cases of permanent neutrality had different purposes and evolution processes, the fact that Swiss neutrality was recommended[32] as the model for neutralisation of Austria points to a robust conceptual connection between the two cases. However, the factors that led to the development of Austrian neutrality and its successful preservation during the Cold War are in many ways different from those observed in the case study of Switzerland.

Since Austrian neutrality, in large part, was the result of a negotiated settlement of a complex political stalemate, the process of establishment of Austrian neutrality can be best explained by examining the highlights of the negotiations among the four powers (the United States, the Soviet Union, the United Kingdom, and France) and the dynamics of international politics that influenced these negotiations in the first decade after the Second World War.

Austrian State Treaty

Austria, also called the Republic of Austria, emerged as an independent state when the Austro-Hungarian Empire dissolved as a result of the Treaty of St. Germain, signed between the allied powers and Vienna on September 1919. The newly created landlocked state of Austria faced serious economic, social, and political challenges, all of which left the country in many ways at the mercy of its powerful neighbour: Germany. As part of his plan to unify all German-speaking populations into the so-called "Greater Germanic Reich", in 1938 Adolf Hitler, the German Chancellor at the time, installed, through intimidation and coercion, a puppet government in Vienna led by Arthur Seyss-Inquart's National Socialist party. The move paved the way for an almost immediate political union (*Anschluss*) between Austria and Germany. Herbert Wright, in his article, "On the Legality of Germany's Annexation of Austria", summarises the apparent ease and haste with which this political union took place: "on the morning of Sunday, March 13, 1938, the Seyss-Inquart Government 'resolved' a Federal Constitutional Law, proclaiming (Art.l) that 'Austria is a state (Land) of the German Reich and providing (Art.2) for a plebiscite on April 10, 1938, on reunion with the German Reich'".[33]

Given that the annexation further strengthened the government of the National Socialist party, ordinary Austrians were in no position to oppose the act and those who did were purged or detained. Germany's annexation of Austria was in clear contradiction of the provisions of the treaties of Versailles and St. Germain which emphasised the protection of independence and territorial integrity of the newly established state of Austria,[34] but European leaders failed to take any concrete action to stop or even oppose it.

It was not until the middle of the Second World War that the foreign ministers of Britain, Russia, and the United States (in a meeting in Moscow in 1943) overruled the *Anschluss* and vowed to re-establish a free and independent Austria after the war ended. However, after its liberation from Nazi Germany in March 1945, Austria was subjected to a supposedly brief military occupation by the four main victors of the Second World War: the Soviet Union, the United States, the United Kingdom, and France. Subsequently, the country, including its capital Vienna, was divided into four zones of control, one for each occupying power.

While the signatories of the joint Four Nations Declaration of 1943 pledged to withdraw their forces swiftly and finalise a "Treaty for Reestablishment of an Independent and Democratic Austria", which later came to be known as the Austrian State Treaty, Gerald Stourzh, an Austrian historian, argues that "the outbreak of the Cold War and the escalation of East–West conflict dimmed expectation of an early conclusion of the treaty and the departure of the foreign military forces".[35] Austria found herself caught in the middle of burgeoning Cold War hostilities, whose main protagonists, the Soviet Union and the United States, had troops stationed on her soil. The fate of Austria's State Treaty and reestablishment of her full sovereignty rested on the outcome of a protracted series of negotiations among the four occupying powers, which continued intermittently between 1947 and 1955. Soviet intransigence, including their initial unequivocal support for Yugoslav's territorial claims against Austria, and interagency disagreement within various US administrations, principally between the State Department and Department of Defense over the context of the treaty and the timeline of its conclusion,[36] seriously overshadowed the negotiations.

At the strategic level, increased tensions between the two camps, the Soviet Union on one side and the Western allies led by the United States on the other side, over issues such as the Berlin blockade, rearmament of a pro-west Federal Republic of Germany, formation of the NATO in 1949 and the Korean War in 1950–1953, further complicated the negotiations and led to the continuation of occupation of Austria for nearly a decade after the Second World War ended.

At the tactical and domestic level, reparations and economic penalties that the Soviet side demanded from Austria were a major bone of contention. For example, the Soviet Union demanded appropriation of all "German assets" in Austria, including the Danube Shipping Company, concessions in all Austrian oil fields, and payment of over a hundred million dollars. The US Government opposed such harsh penalties knowing that as the Austrian Government and the rest of its allies were unwilling and unable fully to comply, the burden of compensation would ultimately fall on the United States.

It appears that the US and some Western governments shared a common concern that a swift conclusion of the State Treaty and a precipitous withdrawal of the Western forces would be a strategic mistake. In the words of Cronin, "an unarmed, economically destitute state, free of the stabilizing influence of four-power occupation, seemed an ideal target for a communist coup—whether organised from within Austria or orchestrated from the Kremlin".[37] Despite this negative attitude and an overall environment of mistrust between the two rival blocks in the late 1940s, Cronin argued that, "at the Paris Conference of Foreign Ministers in June 1949, Soviet policy appeared to provide an unprecedented opportunity for a treaty, albeit on economic terms favorable to the USSR".[38]

The opportunity arose due to a rift between Stalin and Tito following which the Soviet side agreed to drop its support for Yugoslavia's territorial claim and eased its demand for reparations, thus creating a unique opening for resolution of the Austrian issue. During the 1949 negotiation, a draft treaty was prepared, which served as the blueprint for the next rounds until it was ultimately signed in 1955.

There was a growing lack of interest in the United States in the early 1950s with respect to the Austrian issue in general, and opposition to provisions of the 1949 draft negotiated State Treaty in particular. As George Kennan, a senior US State Department official, noted, "the USA no longer felt bound to the items of the State Treaty that had been arranged".[39] During this period, particularly after the outbreak of the Korean War, the US administration focused more on arming and training the pro-West Austrian army than on diplomatic efforts to end the occupation of Austria. Arguing on the merit of Austria's strategic location and its overland transit route connecting West Germany to Italy, Cronin maintains that Admiral Arthur Radford, Chairman of the Joint Chiefs of Staff, advised against acceptance of a treaty which could lead to neutralisation of Austria.[40] While the top brass in the US military preferred the status quo to neutralisation, some planners even encouraged inclusion of Austria into NATO.

The turn of events in early 1953 spurred renewed optimism for a thaw in East–West rivalry and opened the way for a possible conclusion of the Austrian State Treaty. The United States inaugurated a new president, Dwight Eisenhower, a former army general, who promoted a pragmatic and flexible foreign policy approach.[41] On the Soviet side, Joseph Stalin's sudden death in March 1953 and changes in the leadership of the Communist

Party, stirred hope for a positive shift in the USSR's foreign policy. It was expected that, unlike their predecessor, new Soviet leaders Malenkov and Khrushchev would adopt an open and accommodative approach toward conduct of the Soviet Union's international relations.

After concluding the armistice that brought an end to the Korean War, President Eisenhower took an active interest in a negotiated settlement of the Austria issue. In his reaction to Stalin's death and the prospect of openness in the USSR's outlook toward the West, President Eisenhower emphasised that "with an Austrian solution, the Soviet Union could show its willingness for a détente".[42] In private, Eisenhower supported a solution based on armed neutrality of Austria, a stand that forced the US military to prepare for such an eventuality and as a result expedite the training and equipping of the Austrian army and gendarmerie.

Initially, the new "collective leadership" in Moscow appeared no less confrontational on major international matters, including an early conclusion of the Austrian State Treaty. The Soviets continued to use the Austrian issue to block rearmament of West Germany and later Germany's entry into NATO. Nevertheless, during this period known as détente, the Soviets started relaxing some of the harsh practices imposed on Austrians who lived in the Soviet zone. For example, restrictions on postal and telephone services were officially removed, strict zonal traffic control was eliminated, and restrictions on movements between the eastern and western parts of Austria were reduced.[43] Perception of change in Soviet foreign policy, particularly among leaders in the West, prompted Prime Minister Churchill to propose a summit conference to discuss major issues facing the two rival blocs. Though they initially refused to include discussion of the Austrian State Treaty in the summit agenda, the Soviets ultimately agreed to resume the debate on Austria and even demanded that an Austrian delegation participate in the upcoming conference in Berlin. The Soviet's gesture raised some hope among the Austrians for an agreement during the Four Powers conference in January 1954.

After two weeks of exhaustive debates over a range of international topics from Far Eastern issues to Indochina, European Defence Community, and disarmament, the Austrian question was the last item to be discussed on 13 February.[44] Given their eagerness for a swift conclusion of the treaty, the Austrian delegation was basically ready, as declared by Foreign Minister Leopold Figl, to "accept every term of the present draft of the State Treaty which would secure Austria's independence, freedom and sovereignty in every respect".[45] The only item to which the Austrian delegation objected as excessive was reparation payment of US$150 million to the Soviet Union, which it demanded be reduced to a more reasonable level. The Western allies also indicated a willingness to assent to most of the Soviet demands raised during the previous rounds of negotiations. However, much to the disappointment of the West and the Austrian delegation, the new Soviet leadership was in no mood for compromise, particularly on issues that could be interpreted as weakness, such as immediate withdrawal from Austria and West Germany's rearmament. Foreign Minister Vyacheslav Molotov proposed insertion of a new article in the Treaty to ensure that "Austria would neither enter into military alliances with other States nor allow the establishment of foreign military bases on [her] territory" and demanded that the withdrawal of troops from Austria take place only after conclusion of a peace treaty with Germany.[46] While these proposals killed any prospect of signing the State Treaty in Berlin, it was the first time that neutralisation officially became a precondition for conclusion of the Austrian State Treaty.

Some Austrian politicians viewed the Soviets' neutrality proposal during the conference in Berlin as a possible compromise solution to end the deadlock; however, it took another year, full of setbacks for Moscow, before the Soviet Union softened its position on the question of Austria. Some scholars argue that the failure to prevent West Germany's accession to NATO and Khrushchev's attempt to present his new "peaceful coexistence" image to the wider world were the main causes behind the reversal of the Soviet position on Austria. In late March 1955, Moscow decided to invite Austrian Chancellor Julius Raab for a bilateral talk on the future of Austria. During a rather brief bilateral negotiation in Moscow, the Soviet side dropped most of its preconditions, such as a German Peace Treaty and assurance against recurrence of *Anschluss*; instead declaration of Austrian neutrality became the Soviet Union's principal condition for conclusion of a treaty.[47]

Despite objections by senior members of the delegation against incorporation of the term *neutrality* in an official document, the Austrian leaders were anxious that failure to reach an agreement could result in a permanent partition of their country between the two superpowers, a situation similar to that of Germany and Korea. Hence, the main goal of the Austrian Government at the time was ending the Four Power occupation and preventing the permanent division of Austria. To achieve this goal, accepting neutrality was a price the Austrians were willing to pay; however as Cronin puts it, "the Austrian delegation agreed to use 'neutrality' on the condition that it be clarified within the declaration. 'Neutrality after the Swiss model' became the agreed formula, and from the time that formula was approved, negotiations proceeded smoothly".[48]

On 15 April 1955, the Moscow Memorandum was signed by the Austrian Chancellor Raab and the Soviet Foreign Minister Molotov in which Austria pledged to become a permanently neutral state. One month later—after another round of brief negotiation among the ambassadors of the four powers in Vienna that produced the final draft—on 15 May 1955, the Austrian State Treaty was signed by the foreign ministers of the four powers.

The conclusion of the Treaty ended the nearly 17-year-long occupation of Austria by foreign forces. On 25 October 1955, the last foreign troops left Austria.[49] The next day (26 October) the Austrian Parliament unanimously endorsed the declaration of Austria's permanent neutrality. The declaration placed particular emphasis on two principles: (1) Austria had declared permanent neutrality of "its own free will" and pledged to defend its neutrality with all available means and (2) Austria would never join any military pacts or allow the creation of foreign military bases on its territory.[50]

Though the Austrian State Treaty declared that the country had opted for permanent neutrality "on its own free will", some scholars argue that Austria, at the time, had limited options, of which neutrality appeared to be the most desirable one. For instance, Black claims that "[Austria] could only choose between continued occupation and permanent neutrality; it did not have the option of an independent foreign policy without obligations".[51] Another eventuality, feared the most by Austrians, was partition of the country between the two rival ideological blocs. Accepting permanent neutrality had thus paved the way for the withdrawal of the occupation forces, guaranteed Austria its full independence, created a buffer zone and reduced the chances of a direct East–West conflict in the region.

Austrian neutrality was also hailed as a major diplomatic victory by both the rival blocs of the Cold War. The West's actual attitude toward the future of Austria could be summarised in a British diplomatic memorandum as early as January 1952 which noted: "a freely chosen neutrality, under which a fully sovereign Austria elect to join no exclusive alliance, might be difficult for us to resist and not incompatible with our vital strategic requirements".[52]

Hence, Western allies considered the withdrawal of the Soviet forces from Austria in the face of West Germany's admission into NATO as a strategic success. At the same time the Soviet Union also claimed that by making Austria a neutral country, it prevented her accession to NATO and absorption in the capitalist world. The Soviet Union apparently perceived that turning Austria into a neutral state through a bilateral initiative would boost the Soviet's image as a "peace-builder" among the undecided, small European and developing nations of Asia and Africa and would promote Khrushchev's new détente approach with the West; hence, a neutral Austria could serve as a stabilising factor in central Europe.

Austria after neutrality

Austria did not face the test of defending its neutrality by all possible means as Switzerland did during the two World Wars. This contributed to Austria's adoption of a policy of active neutrality by subsequently joining the United

Nations and the Council of Europe, and participating in the UN peacekeeping missions in contrast to Switzerland's pursuit of a conservative and strict form of neutrality.

Austria successfully maintained its policy of neutrality throughout the rough years of the Cold War. The only serious, though manageable, challenge Austrian neutrality faced was in the aftermath of the Hungarian crisis of 1956, when more than170,000 refugees entered the country. Austria's response to the crisis remained within the boundary of humanitarian action; however, the Soviet Union and her Warsaw Pact allies accused the Austrian Government of "having allowed 'reactionary elements' and weapons to cross the Austrian-Hungarian border and thus of having violated its neutrality".[53] While the majority of the Austrian people expressed sympathy with the revolutionary Hungarians, the government in Vienna upheld its promise of neutrality and the crisis passed without jeopardising Austria's neutrality.

Austria, similar to Switzerland, proved useful as a source of information and hub for back-channel contacts between the superpowers.[54] Vienna became the host city for the headquarters of a number of UN and multilateral organisations such as the offices of the International Atomic Energy Agency (IAEA), the Organization of the Petroleum Exporting Countries (OPEC), the United Nations Industrial Development Organization (UNIDO), and the United Nations Office on Drugs and Crime (UNODC).

Austria maintained her tradition of neutrality, even after the fall of the communist bloc in the early 1990s. Notwithstanding certain tendencies and deliberations on the possibility of acquiring NATO membership in 1995–1996, public opinion surveys showed that for Austrians, neutrality is one of the most significant aspects of their identity. Abandoning neutrality, as argued by Andras Kovacs and Ruth Wodak, "is not a matter of any calculation based in realpolitik but a decision that concerns the strongest pillar of Austrian post-war identity."[55]

Analysis of Austrian neutrality

The case study of Austrian neutrality offers necessary insight to test the applicability of the proposed analytical framework.

External factors/variables

Geopolitical position and importance

Austria, in the early 1950s, with a population of roughly seven million, an annual per capita GDP of less than US$1,000, modest natural resource endowments, and, at best, a trivial impact on the international system, qualified as a small state in both absolute and relative terms. Geographically, Austria was located on the borderline between the Eastern and Western blocs in Europe during the Cold War. While the western parts of Austria were of a certain strategic significance to NATO's ability to defend its southern flank, particularly by connecting West Germany to Italy, its eastern parts, including its capital and most populated city, Vienna, were surrounded by the Warsaw Pact nations.[56] Each rival military pact had clear defence advantages only in their contiguous areas, NATO in the West and Warsaw in the East. For both sides, the cost of occupation and forward defence of Austria seemed more than the strategic benefit of controlling it. Hence, Austria's buffer geography and her marginal geopolitical significance at the time corresponds with the first precondition of a viable neutrality set forth in the analytical framework and made the country a suitable candidate for neutrality.

Dynamics of external powers' conflict and competition

Since Austria did not experience active conflict during the presence of the Soviet and Western military forces inside the country, neutrality, in large part, could be seen as an instrument of conflict prevention, mainly aimed at removing the country from an area of potential superpower confrontation.

While there were a number of other external and domestic motivations discussed throughout the case study that led to the creation of consensus on Austrian neutrality, existence of a global balance of power (or terror) between the Cold War rival blocs in the early 1950s was certainly one among the major factors that contributed to Austrian neutrality. At the strategic level, a situation of stable nuclear deterrence or a "balance of terror" emerged after the Soviet Union acquired deployable nuclear weapons. Furthermore, victory of communists in China in 1949 and military stalemate during the first Cold War confrontation in the Korean peninsula produced a balance of power between the East and the West.

Inside Austria, neither the Western allies nor the Soviet Union were in a position to escalate the hostilities or indefinitely sustain a high-level military presence. On the Western side, under strong domestic and economic strain, France and the United Kingdom were in favour of an early withdrawal. Indeed, by the end of 1954, according to Cronin, "the French had almost completely withdrawn their forces from Austria ... and the British had cut their strength down to one battalion".[57] By this time, even President Eisenhower in private exchanges acknowledged that armed neutrality similar to the Swiss model offered an opportunity for breaking the deadlock over the Austrian State Treaty, and that the United States would have no objections if such a deal could guarantee an immediate withdrawal of Soviet forces from Austria.

Similarly, for the Soviet Union, the unrest in East Germany and Czechoslovakia in 1953–1954 put a strain on already overstretched Soviet military and economic resources. On the other hand, the Soviet Union had already consolidated its presence in Hungary and Romania from where it could project power inside Austria, particularly in its eastern part, if needed. However, to counter the US-sponsored NATO alliance, assure its Eastern European allies, and reinforce the balance of power in the region, the Soviet Union established the Warsaw military pact in 1955.

As indicated in the analytical framework, systemic factors, such as the emergence of an overall power balance, coupled with the high cost and limited strategic significance of controlling Austria by the superpowers, created a military stalemate: a situation necessary for adoption of neutrality. Yet in this case, it was the reduction of hostilities and emergence of the East–West détente in Europe that produced an environment conducive to building consensus among the great powers on the neutralisation of Austria.

Consensus and agreement of neighbouring countries and the Great Powers

In the case of Austria, the broad consensus among major stakeholders—the four occupation powers—on neutralisation as a compromised solution had both material and ideational roots.

Generally, by late 1953, the United States and its allies shared a common affirmative position vis-à-vis a neutral Austria if it was the only condition for conclusion of the State Treaty and withdrawal of the Soviet forces. In his statement during the 1954 Berlin conference of foreign ministers, US Secretary of State John Foster Dulles insisted that "a neutral status is an honourable status if it is voluntarily chosen by a nation ... Austria would be free to choose for itself to be a neutral state like Switzerland. Certainly the United States would fully respect its choice".[58] The main source of Western opposition to neutralisation of Austria was that "it might set [a] precedent for Germany". Therefore the West's insistence on the Swiss model during the Foreign Minister's conference in Berlin, according to Stourzh, was to "deflect the neutrality issue away from Germany to the level of small countries".[59] To this end, the Western allies intensified their efforts to integrate the Federal Republic of Germany into a military alliance before fully acceding to a neutrality-based solution for Austria.

Accordingly, the Soviet leadership, particularly after Stalin's death, were convinced that Austria was not going to become a satellite socialist state. Moscow wanted to use the Austrian issue to prevent West Germany's rearmament and accession into Western military alliances. However, when finally, on 23 October 1954, the Paris agreement paved the way for West

Germany to join NATO, the Soviet Union lost its most convincing rationale for delaying the conclusion of the Austrian State Treaty.

Austrian neutrality arguably stemmed from Khrushchev's idea and initiative to promote a détente in Europe.[60] Hence the case of Austrian neutralisation had both the consensus and formal agreement among the great powers.

Domestic factors

Stability and cohesion

Austria did not experience violence after the country was liberated in May 1945. The occupation forces were initially responsible for all security matters in their area of control; however, the Austrian state agencies gradually assumed responsibility of routine civil services. On 25 November 1945, the Austrians held their first post-war election and the two major parties, the Austrian People's Party (ÖVP) and the Socialist Party of Austria (SPÖ), formed a unity government. Hence, within less than six months of her liberation, Austria owned a politically legitimate and popular state.

Withdrawal of the occupation forces and restoration of Austrian sovereignty was the main obsession of the Austrian political leadership. When conclusion of the State Treaty was overshadowed and complicated by the East–West rivalry, permanent neutrality began to emerge as a possible compromise outcome.

The notion of "military non-alignment" entered into the discourse over Austria's future in the early 1950s. Stourzh points to a statement by Theodor Koerner, Austria's second president, who in February 1952 suggested that "Switzerland would be a model for a free Austria".[61] But it was only after the election of Julius Raab as Chancellor in 1953 and increased frustration with lack of serious attention on the part of the Western allies that the Austrian Government earnestly began to break the stalemate. Raab's government opened bilateral back channels[62] with the Soviet Union and offered to accept permanent neutrality as a condition for full sovereignty. The Moscow Memorandum, which proposed Swiss-style neutrality and paved the way for conclusion of the State Treaty, was a product of bilateral negotiations between a popularly elected Austrian Government and the Soviet Union. Therefore, at the domestic level, permanent neutrality of Austria became possible as a result of popular support reflected in a unified action by the two major political parties, the ÖVP and the SPÖ. Based on the above analysis, it is fair to argue that in 1955 Austria possessed sufficient domestic political stability and social cohesion to embrace and maintain permanent neutrality.

Military and economic capabilities

Post-1945 Austria had neither the military nor the economic capabilities stated above. The economy was devastated during the war and suffered from a colonial-style exploitation by the occupation forces in the immediate aftermath of the war. In the summer of 1947, Austria faced a food shortage crisis that resulted in violent riots in Vienna.[63] However, in the early 1950s, the economy swiftly recovered, and in the next five years, Austria experienced a steady growth, thanks to a generous Marshall Plan aid package and the deft economic and industrial reform efforts of the Austrian Government.[64] While in the initial post-war years the Austrian economy was overly reliant on foreign aid where the foreign aid to GDP ratio was over 10 per cent, by 1953 this share dropped to below 2 per cent. In 1955, when Austria declared its permanent neutrality, the country had a functioning infrastructure, a productive industry, a healthy balance of payment, and above all, a per capita real GDP of US$5,053.[65]

The level of economic strength enjoyed by Austria at the time was well above the minimum threshold set by our analysis framework. Moreover, with conclusion of the State Treaty, Austria re-claimed around 450 firms, including substantial oil production and transportation firms in the eastern region. This expanded its industrial base and further strengthened the economy.

From the legal point of view, permanent neutrality has to be internationally recognised and acknowledged; hence the four signatories and later all members of the UN Security Council recognised Austria's declaration of neutrality. However, it was made clear in the State Treaty that defending and preserving permanent neutrality was the sole responsibility of the Austrian Government. Articles 13 and 14 of the Treaty envisioned the creation of the Austrian armed forces and allowed Austria to use the remaining German war materials to equip its forces. In fact, lack of a credible force in the words of Rathkolb to "suppress a domestic Communist coup d'état and delay an attack from the Eastern bloc through Austrian territory"[66] was one of the main reasons why the US Government was initially against the idea of Austria's neutrality.

In the early 1950s, the US military began to establish a small pro-Western Austrian gendarmerie; however, after the conclusion of the Treaty, the United States alone invested a total of US$136 million for equipping and training a 28,000-strong Austrian armed force.[67] During the same period, Austria also formed a modest Air Force to guard its air space. However, in general, as explained by Oliver Rathkolb, the Austrian forces followed a doctrine of deterrence and "began to reorganize on the basis of guerrilla warfare combined with overall defence of the Austrian society and Austrian social partners in order to 'lengthen' an attack. It would cost the aggressor too much time and too many dead soldiers to break through Austrian territory".[68]

Austrian political leadership recognised the significance of military preparedness for maintenance of neutrality, and, in the words of Bruno Kreisky, State Secretary for Foreign Affairs, "Austria followed the example of Sweden and Switzerland, both of which hold to the view that military non-alignment necessarily involves the creation of a certain military potential commensurate with the country's strategic position … such measures as Austria did take have proved beyond doubt that it is a country that means to defend its territory".

Summary

Austria has certainly been a success story in the application of permanent neutrality in the international system. Permanent neutrality served the interests of both external and internal stakeholders in the struggle over the fate of post-Second World War Austria. The policy reduced the probability of East–West conflict inside Austria, paved the way for a face-saving withdrawal of the occupation forces, and guaranteed return of full sovereignty to the Austrian people.

As observed, the presence of these five external and domestic factors can in large extent explain the success and sustainability of Austrian permanent neutrality. However, the examination of Austrian neutrality presents an additional crucial factor, as also noted by Cronin,[69] necessary for the viability of permanent neutrality. It is the existence of fixed borders, accepted by both the great powers and by the candidate/neutral state, as well as the absence of expansionist and irredentist ambitions on the part of the candidate and the neighbouring states.[70]

The case study of Laos

The Declaration of Neutrality of Laos signed in Geneva in July 1962 by 14 stakeholder states represented a major international attempt to apply permanent neutrality as a diplomatic tool to end the conflict in Laos.[71] It was also the first instance in which a policy of permanent neutrality was applied outside Europe and in a situation where the number of stakeholders was larger and more diverse than in any other previous case. The text—a product of more than 14 months of strenuous negotiations among the three rival Lao factions and their regional and international backers— scrupulously outlined the obligation of the parties and its enforcement mechanism.

While high-level Lao officials had used Switzerland as an example when defining the nature of their neutrality,[72] it seems more likely that a successful neutralisation of Austria in 1955 might have encouraged the Cold War rivals to apply the policy to the conflict in Laos. In terms of its purpose and processes, there are a number of similarities between the permanent neutrality of Laos and that of Austria. In both cases, permanent neutrality was an outcome of a negotiated settlement through a prolonged and complex multilateral mechanism. Similarly, given the geopolitical constraints of the Cold War era and their regional problems, neither country had easy alternatives to accepting an internationally endorsed neutralisation. Additionally, Austria and Laos also shared the common feature of being "side shows" to more important theatres of the Cold War era: the struggle over the future of Germany in Europe and the Vietnam War in Southeast Asia, respectively. Ultimately, in both cases, the signatories offered only nominal and non-binding promises, not guaranteeing the sovereignty and permanent neutrality of the candidate states but committing to respect them. Since the onus of upholding neutrality was on the subject states, Austria—a state with strong social, political, and economic institutions—managed to maintain and make best of its neutrality while, by contrast, Laos—a weak, divided, and poor French colony—failed to do so.

Notwithstanding the meticulous details with which the declaration on neutrality of Laos was crafted, and despite certain similarities between Austria and Laos, the instrument of permanent neutrality failed to stabilise Laos and remove it from the wider conflict in Southeast Asia. The main goal of this case study is to evaluate the dynamics of Laotian neutrality and to examine the reasons for its failure in the light of the five factors described in the analytical framework.

A prelude to the permanent neutrality of Laos

According to Martin Stuart-Fox, a journalist and expert on Laotian history, the modern history of Laos as a nation state begins in 1945.[73] However, the creation of present-day Laos begins from 1893, after France wrested the control of territories on the east of the Mekong River from Siam and annexed them with her Indochina colonies.

The French adopted an indirect and loose governing system in which the central Laos region of Laung Prabang was administrated by King Sisavang Vong and the southern and northern regions were run by senior French officials often assisted by the Vietnamese bureaucrats and in some areas by members of local Lao aristocracy.

In April 1945, King Sisavang Vong, under pressure from Japanese occupation forces, proclaimed Lao independence from France.[74] Following the end of the Second World War, Prince Phetsarath Ratanavongsa, the Prime Minister and Viceroy of Laos, supported by a group of nationalists, who later led the Lao Issara (Free Lao) movement, and encouraged by France's defeat both in Europe and in Indochina, reaffirmed the April royal proclamation of independence from France.[75] However, Sisavang Vong, the pro-France monarch, now free from Japanese coercion, swiftly opposed nationalist calls for independence. Instead, he wanted Laos to become a constitutional monarchy under an overall French suzerainty.

When King Sisavang Vong rejected Prince Phetsarath's call for independence and stripped him of his royal title, the nationalists established a defence committee and announced the creation of a Lao Issara government in Vientiane, the future capital city of Laos. Prince Souvanna Phouma was appointed the Minister of Public Works and his younger half-brother, Souphanouvong, who had the support of the Vietnamese resistance forces—the Viet Minh—became the Defence Minister.

The French reinforcement contingent was sent to restore the colonial administration in Laos and support King Sisavang Vong who was isolated in his royal seat in Laung Prabang. The French easily defeated the ill-equipped Lao Issara government, incorporated the southern fiefdom of Champassak and offered its ruler, Prince Boun Oum, a senior position in the central government. Soon the French re-established their control over the entire territory of Laos and reinstated King Sisavang Vong as the nominal ruler of the whole kingdom.

Lao Issara leadership escaped to Siam and continued their political and military resistance against the French occupation from across the border. Differences of opinion over methods of achieving independence grew more visible among the exiled leadership of Lao Issara in Bangkok. Phetsarath remained convinced that reconciliation and a political rapprochement with the King were possible; therefore, he signalled his intention to return to Laos if the King reinstated his title as Viceroy. While his younger brother Souvanna Phouma also preferred a political solution over armed resistance, he, however, was more concerned with independence and constitutional reform as a precondition for his cooperation with the Royal government.

Souphanouvong, the youngest and more left-leaning half-brother, took a more hard-line revolutionary approach *vis-à-vis* the resolution of conflict in Laos. When removed from Lao Issara for his uncompromising stand and overreliance on the Viet Minh, he established his own political and military entity called the Progressive People's Organization, later known as Pathet Lao (Lao Nation). This paramilitary organisation continued to harass French forces in the Vietnam-Laos border regions.

After a Franco-Lao General Convention conceded greater autonomy to Laos in the summer of 1949, Souvanna Phouma and a dozen Lao Issara leaders decided to return home and work with the Royal government in Vientiane. In the autumn of 1951, Souvanna Phouma became the Prime Minister of Laos and for the next three years, he intensified political pressure on the French Government to attain Laos's full independence. On 15 October 1953, France finally recognised the Kingdom as a fully independent and sovereign state and a treaty of amity and cooperation was signed between the two nations.[76]

While the post-Second World War era opened a window of opportunity for Laos to build a modern nation state, sharp political disagreements among ambitious rival "Princes", together with continued interference by stronger neighbours, poverty, lack of resources, and finally Laos's geopolitical position at the fault line of the Cold War, placed the country on a trajectory of prolonged civil strife and proxy wars for the next three decades.

The conflict in Laos was mainly connected to a more complex struggle, fought first between France and the Vietnamese guerrillas (1946–1954) and later between the United States and its allies, and the North Vietnamese Government and its supporters (1955–1975). Hence, simply put, Laos, itself not a major player in the conflict, was caught in the middle of others' wars. The most logical response in such circumstances in the toolkit of diplomatic solutions therefore was to remove Laos from the middle of the conflict by making it a neutral state.

Historically, such a solution had worked with various degrees of success in Europe. However, as we will see in the next section, the complexity of the situation, particularly the multitude of actors and the divergence of interest in the conflict in Southeast Asia, set the limits of neutralisation as a generally applicable diplomatic solution to the conflict in small buffer states.

The intricate and interconnected nature of the conflict in Laos, with respect to the larger conflict in Southeast Asia, demands that the subject be discussed in greater detail than the previous case studies. To this end, the study examines the internal and external dynamics of the conflict in Laos in two stages: first, the era of voluntary neutrality from 1954 to 1963 and second, the period of permanent neutrality from 1963 to 1975.

Independence and voluntary neutrality

By early 1954, the conflict between French forces and Vietnamese guerrillas intensified and culminated in a humiliating defeat for French expeditionary forces in Dien Bien Phu, a valley near the Vietnam-Laos border. The ultimate surrender of nearly 10,000 French forces to the Viet Minh marked the end of French colonial authority in Indochina. The episode flared international tensions and placed the region under a new spotlight. In May

1954, major regional and international stakeholders gathered in Geneva to work out a diplomatic solution to the conflict in Indochina. Under a joint British and Soviet chair, the participants, after nearly four months of intense negotiation, produced an agreement also known as the Geneva Accords. The document called for the cessation of hostilities in Vietnam, divided the country (provisionally) along the seventeenth parallel into two zones of control, demanded withdrawal of Viet Minh and other communist forces and guerrillas from Laos and Cambodia, and stipulated holding free and fair elections in the next two years in each country.[77] While the Geneva Accords reiterated Laos's unity, sovereignty, and independence, Phoui Sananikone, leader of the Laotian delegation in the conference, unilaterally declared that:

> Laos will never join in any agreement with other states if this agree-ment includes the obligation for the Royal Government of Laos to participate in a military alliance not in conformity with Charter of the United Nations or the with the principles of the agreement on the ces-sation of hostilities or, unless its security is threatened, the obligation to establish bases on the territory of Laos or military forces of the foreign Powers.[78]

The government of Laos further pledged not to seek foreign military or economic aid beyond what had been stipulated in the agreement for training the Royal Lao Army. This voluntary commitment, in essence, amounted to a unilateral declaration of neutrality, a position strongly championed and pursued by Prime Minister Souvanna Phouma.

Under the terms of the Geneva Accords, the Royal government agreed to include members of the Pathet Lao in senior administrative positions and allow its forces to regroup in the two northern provinces of Phong Saly and Sam Neua. The agreement emphasised that the arrangement was limited to the period between the ceasefire and the general election planned for 1955. The Accords also envisaged an International Control Commission consist-ing of Canada, India, and Poland to monitor and supervise the implementa-tion of its provision in Laos and Vietnam.

The initial provisions of the agreement concerning cessation of hostili-ties, withdrawal of Viet Minh forces, and regrouping of Pathet Lao fight-ers in the two designated provinces were partially fulfilled. However, complete reintegration of Pathet Lao forces into the Royal Army, termi-nation of the Viet Minh incursion into Laos, and conducting a free and fair election proved more challenging in practice. Despite a brief disrup-tion in political negotiation and boycotting of the 1955 election by Pathet Lao, the two brothers, Prime Minister Souvanna Phouma and Pathet Lao leader Souphanouvong, finally met on August 1956 and agreed to create an inclusive government. With the formation of a unity government and the holding of assembly elections in 1957 and 1958, the Laotian Government announced the conclusion of the Geneva agreements and termination of the mission of the International Commission for Supervision and Control in Laos (ICC). However, the ensuing incidents proved that the claims were premature and naïve.

What the historians of Laos call the First Coalition (1957–1958) lasted for almost a year before it collapsed due to increasing domestic and foreign pressure. Domestically, the idea of political accommodation of Pathet Lao and their increasing clout in the government united anti-communist hardliners into an army-supported right-wing political group known as the Committee for the Defence of the National Interest, or CDNI.

Given the army's strong connections and its reliance on the West, the journalist Stuart-Fox blames "US machinations" for the collapse of the first coalition government and the subsequent instability in Laos. He argues that the United States viewed Prime Minister Souvanna Phouma's reconciliation efforts as helping the ascendency of communism in Southeast Asia. Stuart-Fox notes that, "[o]bsessed by the Cold War and sceptical of Lao capacity to manage their own affairs, US policymakers in Washington were horrified by the turn of events".[79]

Between 1959 and 1962, Laos entered a period of instability marked by the breakdown of reconciliation and reintegration processes, coups and counter-coups, civil war, and increasing foreign intervention. After the resignation of Souvanna Phouma and the collapse of his coalition government, the United States took an active role in supporting the anti-communist Phoui Sananikone's government. The United States expanded its economic and military support to Laos. While US officials continued to use the logic of containment of communism and support for non-communist forces against expansion of Soviet and Chinese influence, the majority of the Laotian people were concerned more about their domestic stability than in containing communism.

Obviously, the introduction of American military advisors to replace French trainers and streaming of US military and consumer supplies into Laos created the issue of "American imperialism" in Laos.[80] Already unhappy with the formation of the Southeast Asia Treaty Organisation (SEATO) and extension of its protective umbrella into Laos, Cambodia, and South Vietnam, Prime Minister Phoui's granting of diplomatic recognition to Taipei and Saigon, and his declaration on termination of the ICC, infuriated Beijing, Moscow, and Hanoi and created grounds for direct intervention from these countries into Laos's internal affairs.

This period also saw the rise of military officers as a third force in the Laotian political arena. These officers and politicians further factionalised the politics of Laos and were responsible for involving the Royal Army in the power struggle in Vientiane. The most notable among them was General Phoumi Nosavan, the Minister of National Defence in Phoui's government. He used his military power to pressurise the King, rig elections, influence the Prime Minister, and chase out Pathet Lao from the political scene. As such, he effectively undermined any prospect of reconciliation with the leftist guerrillas.

While initially a staunch anti-communist supported by Field Marshal Sarit Thanarat, the Prime Minister of Thailand, the US military, and the CIA, General Phoumi later became an obstacle to reaching a political solution when President John F. Kennedy sought to encourage Laos's neutrality and the formation of a coalition government.

Another important military officer who emerged on the political scene in the early 1960s was Captain Kong Le, commander of an elite second paratroop battalion in the capital. On 8 August 1961, when the entire Royal Lao cabinet was in Laung Prabang to meet the new King, Sisavang Vatthana, Captain Le staged a *coup d'état* and overthrew the right-wing government put together by General Phoumi. The coup, which restored the neutralist Sovanna Phouma as the Prime Minister, had an anti-US flavour.

In the early 1960s the country was divided among three hostile forces, namely, the government of Prime Minister Souvanna Phouma supported by Captain Le (the neutralists); General Phoumi's military and political allies, including their southern loyalist (the rightists); and the Pathet Lao (the leftists). Besides the traditional outside backers of each rival group (the US and Thailand, on one side, and China and North Vietnam, on the other side), following the establishment of its embassy in Vientiane in October 1960, the Soviet Union also began supporting Prime Minister Souvanna Phouma and Captain Kong Le's neutralist forces. With such a dangerous configuration of domestic and outside forces, which according to historian Arthur Dommen changed "the entire complexion of the Laos confrontation",[81] the country was heading toward a bloody civil war.

The chaos in Laos was further exacerbated when the United States and Thailand recognised General Phoumi's self-appointed government in Vientiane, and the communist countries continued to recognise the neutralist government of Souvanna Phouma, which retreated to the Khang Khy province. In this period Laos was rapidly becoming an active frontline of the Cold War in Southeast Asia. For example, by 1961, besides countless irregular North Vietnamese forces that were fighting alongside the Pathet Lao, according to Roland Paul, there were an estimated 700 US and 500 Soviet forces inside Laos supporting the warring sides.[82]

The deterioration of the situation in Southeast Asia, particularly in Laos, once again drew the attention of major powers in search for ways of "defusing what threatened to become a serious international crisis".[83] A number of stakeholders, such as Britain, India, and the Soviet Union, proposed convening an international conference to seek a comprehensive solution to the conflict in Laos, which by that time had acquired new dimensions.

Meanwhile, John F. Kennedy, the newly sworn US President, sought to disengage from conflict in Laos at the earliest opportunity. Kennedy announced that the United States "'strongly and unreservedly' supported 'the goal of a neutral and independent Laos'".[84] To explore the possibilities of a negotiated settlement, Kennedy appointed Ambassador Averell Harriman as a special envoy to Laos. In a June 1961 summit with Soviet leader Nikita Khrushchev in Vienna, President Kennedy reiterated his administration's support for "constructive negotiations" among the main stakeholders to end the conflict and restore Laos's "genuine neutrality". Apparently at this stage neither the United States nor the Soviet Union saw key strategic interests at play in Laos. The leaders, hence, agreed that a negotiated settlement was in both countries' interests, and that a unified, independent, and neutralised Laos should emerge.[85] This superpower consensus was the main force behind an intensified effort to find a diplomatic solution to the conflict in Laos.

At the initiative of Britain and the Soviet Union, an international conference on the Laotian question began on 16 May 1961. The negotiations among representatives of three belligerent parties, the right-wing Phoumist, the neutralists, and the communist Pathet Lao, as well as major regional and international stakeholders, continued for over a year.

While talks continued in Geneva, and occasionally other Swiss cities, the belligerent Lao factions were trying to gain the upper hand in the negotiations by acquiring new territories in the battlefield. In May 1962 all parties ultimately consented to a three-way coalition government that paved the way for conclusion of stalled talks in Geneva and signing of the final declaration.[86]

On 23 July 1962, high representatives of Burma, Cambodia, Canada, China, Democratic Republic of Vietnam, France, India, Poland, Republic of Vietnam, Thailand, the Soviet Union, the United Kingdom, and the United States signed the Declaration and Protocol on the Neutrality of Laos.[87]

Article 4 of the Declaration stated that the Royal Government of Laos:

> will not enter into any military alliance or into any agreement, whether military or otherwise, which is inconsistent with the neutrality of the Kingdom of Laos; it will not allow the establishment of any foreign military base on Laotian territory, nor allow any country to use Laotian territory for military purposes of interference in the internal affairs of

other countries, nor recognize the protection of any alliance or military coalition, including SEATO.

The declaration also acknowledged the abrogation of all previous treaties and agreements that contradicted the principles of neutrality. The signatories of the documents, on their part, committed to respecting Laotian sovereignty and territorial integrity, and not to use the territory of Laos to interfere in the affairs of other countries. In paragraph 4, the participants also pledged to:

> Undertake, in the event of a violation or threat of violation of the sovereignty, independence, neutrality, unity or territorial integrity of the Kingdom Laos, to consult jointly with the Royal Government of Laos and among themselves in order to consider measures which might prove to be necessary to ensure the observance of these principles and the other provisions of the present Declaration.

The attached Protocol to the Declaration called for the withdrawal of all "foreign regular and irregular troops, foreign para-military formations and foreign military personnel in the shortest time possible".[88] A revamped International Commission for Supervision and Control in Laos was tasked to monitor the withdrawal of all foreign personnel and full implementation of the documents.

In terms of its details and nuances, the declaration was the most comprehensive document on neutrality to date; in practice, given the complexity of the situation in the region, the whole deal, according to Roland, was nothing more than an "ambiguous compromise set forth in rather unambiguous language in the Declaration on the Neutrality of Laos and the Protocol to that Declaration, signed by 13 communist and non-communist countries in July 1962".[89]

The agreements helped in the establishment of a "unity government" with neutralist Souvanna Phouma as Prime Minister. General Phoumi and Prince Souvannvong each secured a Deputy Prime Minister portfolio and the rest of the ministerial positions were distributed among the three factions. With the formation of an internationally sanctioned and inclusive government, a general sense of optimism prevailed among the Lao people. However, fulfilling the provision of the Geneva agreements and turning Laos into a truly neutral state proved to be a daunting challenge. The country was *de facto* divided among three forces, who maintained their own armies and parallel administrations. Skirmishes among them were a daily routine.

The immediate task of the new government was to demobilise the three separate armed forces and reintegrate them into a Royal Laos Army, reform economic and fiscal policies, and above all establish a balanced relationship with its neighbours. Prime Minister Souvanna Phouma attached a higher priority to rebalancing Lao's foreign relations by granting diplomatic recognition to the People's Republic of China and improving ties with North Vietnam. The new government also enjoyed a warm relationship with the Kennedy Administration. It established new diplomatic relationships with a number of Eastern European countries. In early 1963, King Savang Vatthana, Prime Minister Souvanna Phouma, and Foreign Minister Quinim Pholsena embarked on a 50-day tour of all signatory nations of the 1962 Geneva Accords. Despite initial success in the domain of foreign relations, deep ideological animosities, personal distrust, and a history of violence among the three opposing factions and disagreements within each faction's leadership meant that progress on the domestic front, particularly with respect to the reconciliation and reintegration efforts, was painstakingly slow. Each side was trying to undercut the other in a bid to increase its own power and reinforce its overall position inside the country.

This resulted in a campaign of political assassinations in early 1963 in which senior cadres of the neutralist and Pathet Lao camps, including Colonel Ketsana and Foreign Minister Pholsena, were murdered. Complaining about lack of security in the capital,[90] Souvannvong and the rest of the Pathet Lao leadership returned to their regional headquarters and resumed their agitations. The neutralists and General Phoumi's rightist forces once again found it convenient to join hands and fight the outgoing communists.

The initial optimism did not last long as the agreements broke down and the coalition government split apart in less than two years. Fighting among the forces of rival groups in the Plains of Jar and several other locations across the country had resumed. Under the pretext of self-defence, the government in Vientiane began to solicit military and financial assistance from the US embassy. The US military advisory team, which was relocated to Thailand after its withdrawal under the terms of the Geneva Accords, increased its support to both General Phoumi and Captain Le's embattled forces.

Beside domestic hostilities and conflicting allegiances of each group, their dependency on outside forces and above all the wider conflict in the region played a significant role in the failure of the Laotian neutrality initiative of 1962. Stuart-Fox succinctly sums up both domestic and external sources of this failure, arguing that:

> the very weakness of Laos made the preservation of neutrality impossible, no matter how many embassies of opposing Cold War antagonists maintained cordial relations with the Royal Lao government in Viang Chang[91]. Moreover, given its strategic position in relation to the antagonistic regimes in North and South Vietnam, even the most

determinedly neutralist government in Laos could do little to enforce its proclaimed neutrality.[92]

A complex mix of hostilities in the surrounding region—for example, between the United States and its SEATO allies and China and North Vietnam, on one hand, and a growing rift between the Soviet Union and China, on the other hand—undermined the prospect of achieving a peaceful resolution to the conflict in Laos through the neutralisation agreement. Recognising the depth of hostilities and the difference in the strategic calculations of the regional powers, Dommen stressed that right from the beginning of the process, "few of the signatories harboured any illusions as to the durability of the settlement at Geneva. Looking ahead beyond the agreement, the Chinese foresaw the complete 'liberation' of Laos, that is, the final elimination from Laos of all Western influence".[93] On the other hand, the United States endorsed Laotian neutrality not only as a policy to avoid further entanglement in the conflict but to hold back the spread of communism in the region. Hence the United States was prepared to offer assistance to strengthen the neutralist government in Vientiane as long as doing so served its policy of containment in the region.

However, during 1964, the conflict in Laos took a new twist when the North Vietnamese built a series of supply routes through Laotian territory to infiltrate the South. In response, the US military heavily bombed these routes and armed the local Hmong minority to disrupt their ground communication. As such, Laos was drawn into the Vietnam War and over the next decade became a battleground of what came to be known as the "Secret War"[94] between the North Vietnamese, Americans, and their local supporters in the region. During this period (1964–1973) the United States dropped over two million tonnes of bombs on Laotian territory, which made it "the most heavily bombed country per capita in history".[95] Stuart-Fox argues that "a decade from 1964 to 1973 Laos was subjected to the most savage warfare in the nation's history".[96]

The US forces withdrew from the region, including Laos, in 1973. In less than two years, the pro-American regimes in Saigon and Vientiane collapsed and fell into the hands of communists in the spring of 1975. In December 1975, Pathet Lao leaders abolished the monarchy and declared the establishment of the Lao People's Democratic Republic. This officially closed the chapter of neutrality in Laos's political history.

Analysis of Laotian neutrality

The failure of neutralisation efforts in Laos offers an interesting contrast to the relative success of neutrality in the Switzerland and Austrian cases. The next section offers an analysis of Laotian neutrality against the external and internal determinants of neutrality suggested in the analytical framework. Given the complex socio-economic and political environment in which it was applied, a careful examination of Laotian neutrality significantly enriches our analytical understanding of the concept and practice of neutrality, and also tests the rigour of the proposed analytical framework.

External factors/variables

Geopolitical position and importance

Geographically, Laos is a small, landlocked state, located at the centre of the Southeast Asia region bordering five larger countries: Thailand, Vietnam, China, Myanmar, and Cambodia. With an area of 236,800 km², a population of nearly 2.4 million, and a per capita GDP of US$692[97] at the time of its neutralisation in 1962, the country was small, vulnerable, and the only landlocked nation in the region. Additionally, for most of its modern history, the country served as buffer state between her powerful neighbours, Thailand and Vietnam, and in the early 1960s it became a battleground for the Cold War in Indochina.[98] While the rival powers were actively involved through proxies and covert operations to deny their opponents' full domination inside Laos, no country was willing to risk another major war, akin to what happened in the Korean peninsula. Jürg Martin Gabriel succinctly describes the US administration's ambivalent attitude toward Laos as follows: "Eisenhower was unprepared to abandon Laos, he was equally unwilling to commit regular American forces".[99] Soviet policy on Laos was mostly directed by its rhetoric of support for revolutionaries around the world rather than being based on strong strategic interest in Laos. It is perhaps an indication that while geopolitically significant to all major powers, Laos was not strategically vital to the interest of the superpowers and therefore suitable for neutralisation.

Dynamics of external powers conflict and competition

The conflict in Laos had at least three, sometimes interconnected, dimensions: domestic, regional, and polar. In the immediate aftermath of the Second World War, the conflict was predominantly rooted in the domestic political differences among the Lao elites on the role of French colonial forces. The disagreement divided the country generally into two large camps: a pro-colonial monarchist camp and a pro-independence constitutionalist camp. From the mid-1950s, particularly after the withdrawal of French forces from the region and the division of Vietnam into a communist

North and a pro-West South, the conflict increasingly acquired a regional dimension with North Vietnam and China actively supporting the Pathet Lao guerrillas in the countryside, and Thailand and South Vietnam helping the Royal government in Vientiane. Ultimately, with the involvement of American, Soviet, and Chinese personnel in the field, particularly from the late 1950s until the withdrawal of most of the US forces from South Vietnam in 1973, Laos became a major battlefield of the Cold War in Southeast Asia.

These three dimensions of the conflict, and the undercurrents within each dimension, make it very difficult to gain a generalisable analysis of the stages and intensity of conflict in Laos, and to argue whether the situation, particularly in the early 1960s, was conducive to neutrality or not. As depicted earlier, in the period preceding the neutralisation agreement of 1962, the situation at the battlefield could roughly be classified as a military stalemate between the Royal Laos Army and the Pathet Lao forces. At the global level, besides the overall balance of power between the Cold War rivals, the American and the Soviet leaders were committed to a neutrality-based diplomatic solution to the conflict in Laos. However, at the regional level, to some players, such as China and North Vietnam, the status quo was far from a stalemate; instead, victory appeared achievable on the battlefield. In such a situation, neutrality may be viewed as a desirable solution by some players but not by others. Therefore, one can argue that at the time of its neutralisation, Laos did not meet the prerequisite of *military stalemate and balance of power* at all levels of the conflict, which resulted in a neutrality agreement signed on paper but not respected on the ground.

Consensus among neighbouring countries and the great powers

The third criterion for successful permanent neutrality is: the emergence of a consensus among the main stakeholders that a solution based on permanent neutrality of the state in question will best serve everyone's relative interests. Such consensus should in turn develop into an internationally endorsed neutrality agreement. With a cursory look at the process of neutralisation of Laos in 1962, one can argue that since a year-long negotiation in Switzerland involved all major stakeholders and resulted in a comprehensive neutrality agreement signed by 14 nations, the case met the third condition of a viable permanent neutrality. However, a deeper look reveals that difference in perceptions, calculations, and incentives, as well as historical rivalries among major stakeholders in the conflict,[100] prevented the emergence of a meaningful consensus among all players. Historical records show that while leaders of the United States and the Soviet Union were in favour of a neutrality-based settlement, regional powers such as China,

North Vietnam, and Thailand did not particularly view neutrality as a viable long-term solution to the conflict in Laos.[101]

While the failure of Laotian neutrality is mostly attributed to the destructive influences of external and systemic factors (such as regional rivalries, the Vietnam War, and the Cold War), domestic issues (such as continuous violence, social fragmentation, and the lack of military and economic capabilities) could also explain, in part, the policy's failure.

Domestic factors/variables

Stability and cohesion

Under our analytical framework, the minimum level of stability required to allow a state to uphold neutrality was defined as *the absence of continuous large-scale violence*. In the case of Laos, despite intermittent ceasefires, the country continued to suffer from severe and prolonged violence. The conflict, which stretched from a limited insurgency after the Second World War into a proxy war and civil war, debilitated the state's authority to provide basic services and maintain law and order.

At the time of its neutralisation in 1962, Laos was already a weak and divided state suffering from persistent violence. The government in Vientiane had no control over large areas of its territory and movements across its border, particularly with North Vietnam. This left the state highly vulnerable to cross-border infiltration and subversion by the neighbouring states and their local agents. Even after the neutrality agreement, assassinations of high-level officials by rival groups, and failure to integrate the three separate armed forces into a national army added to state fragility and rendered neutrality inadequate to function as a source of stability and cohesion. Furthermore, the presence of North Vietnamese, American, Chinese, and Russian "advisors" was both the cause and a consequence of instability and violence in the country. Anoulak Kittikhoun described the dynamic of external intervention and its impact on domestic politics of Laos as follows: "the clash between the US and communist Soviet Union and China had a particular logic that resulted in especially acute and ceaseless interventions in the region that compromised the ability of different Lao factions to form coalition governments and prevent revolutionary takeover".[102]

In terms of its social cohesion, Hugh Toye argued:

> Laos as formed by the French was unstable because it included mutually hostile ethnic elements closely connected with the population it was required to separate. The dominant Lao valley people feared and

disliked the Vietnamese, as did their Lao neighbours in north-east Siam. The hill folk in upper Laos, on the other hand, disliked the Laos and tended to look for support towards their close kinsmen across the border in North Vietnam.[103]

In such an environment, no matter how diligent the neutrality agreement was, and how committed the superpowers appeared, the Laotian state was unable to bring stability and implement the provisions of the neutrality agreement.

As mentioned previously, in some instances the idea of neutrality functions as a source of domestic consensus and helps in building social cohesion. For example, in the case of Switzerland, neutrality became a source of social cohesion and national identity manifested in the creation of the Confederation. Also, in post-Second World War Austria, the idea of neutrality developed into a basis for political consensus and a means to a greater end of regaining full sovereignty. Such political consensus was arguably reflected in the formation of a pro-neutrality grand coalition government in 1953.

In Laos, however, the ideal of neutrality failed to become either a source of social cohesion or a basis for political consensus for building a stable and prosperous nation. Instead, it became an end by itself. As the case study indicates, initially a group of the members of the political elite led by Prime Minister Souvanna Phouma embraced a "position of complete neutrality like Switzerland's"[104] as a political ideal and as a means of removing Laos from the arena of confrontation among the great powers. A prominent historian of Laos, Arthur Dommen, echoed this sentiment by emphasising that "the survival of a Laos that is neither a colonial possession occupied by European or American garrisons nor a Vietnamese fief in a Communist-dominated Indochinese federation, nor a vassal of a powerful and expansionist China, depends on the effective neutralization of Laos by international consent".[105] However, given that the country was already divided between two strong ideological fronts—the urban-dwelling rightists and monarchists, and the younger, educated leftist supported by masses of peasants in remote areas— at the grassroots level, support for neutrality was limited and both sides viewed it with suspicion. Social fragmentation amongst the tribal groups, and ideological propaganda, mostly by communist activists, prevented the emergence of a national consensus on neutrality.

Hence, despite international attempts, neutrality, as an ideal for social cohesion and a means for political solution, failed to take root in Laotian society. Instead, neutrality morphed into an ideological base for a separate political party, the neutralists, which presided over several weak coalition governments until the fall of Vientiane to communist forces in 1975.

Military and economic capabilities

As argued in the analytical framework, maintenance of neutrality is directly linked to a state's military and economic capabilities. Militarily, the candidate for neutrality has to be able to inflict substantial cost and deny the potential aggressors an overall victory. Economically, the state should at least be able to maintain its military and civilian administration, and should not be overly dependent on financial and material support from foreign sources.

A closer observation of post-independence Laos reveals that the country did not meet either condition. At the time of the first Geneva Declaration in 1954, the total strength of the Laotian Armed Forces was estimated at around 15,000 men. The force, created by the Colonial French Administration as a future police force, remained highly dependent on France for leadership and technical and logistical support, and was incapable of independently securing the country.[106] Bernard Fall describes the forces as follows: "[w]hat the French left to defend the Kingdom against the Pathet Lao and North Vietnamese was but a native militia".[107] Recognising their acute inability to maintain law and order inside Laos, the signatories of the 1954 Geneva Declaration provisioned 1,500 French military officers to train the Royal Lao Armed Forces and another 3,500-strong force to assist in defence matters.

The training and support missions did not materialise as planned due to the political and economic pressures facing France at home, and the insurgency in Algeria. Meanwhile, on the ground, the poorly trained and ill-equipped Royal Lao Army was often humiliated by Pathet Lao insurgents and their Vietnamese supporters, which further weakened its morale and standing as a professional army.

The United States stepped in to fill the gap. By 1959, the strength of the Royal Army grew to 25,000 men and subsequently to 29,000. According to a Congressional Committee Report, the US Government funded Laos's entire military budget and a large portion of its civilian spending.[108] However, American training and equipping was geared more toward fighting the spread of communism in the region than toward preparing the Royal Army to preserve the country's neutrality. This irritated the regional powers, such as China and North Vietnam, who in turn increased their subversive activities. Dependency on US funding also influenced the political orientation of the Royal Army's leadership and caused ideological differences among its cadres, ultimately dividing the armed forces into pro-US and pro-neutrality camps. The 1960s military coup by neutralist Captain Kong Le, the counter-coup by rightist General Phoumi, and the subsequent infighting between their forces across the country further debilitated the army's strength and its position among ordinary people.

On the economic side, landlocked, sparsely populated, and with a per capita GDP of around US$630 in the 1950s, Laos was one of the poorest countries in Southeast Asia. The country lacked basic infrastructure, such as all-weather roads, electricity generation capacity, irrigation systems, and railways. It hardly produced any industrial goods and over 90 per cent of its population was engaged in subsistence farming. Similar to its military sector, Laos's economy was also reliant on foreign aid on a scale that Jean Pierre Barbier, a French scholar and official in Vientiane in the early 1970s, described as "un pays malade de l'aide eternagere, or a country made sick by foreign assistance".[109] According to data from the US Agency for International Development, between 1955 and 1963, total US foreign aid to Laos reached an amount of US$481 million, which made the country the largest per capita recipient of US aid in the entire region.[110] Two-thirds of the aid money went to salaries of the army and civilian administration, one-third was used for provision of military equipment, and very little, if any at all, went to building infrastructure or improving agricultural productivity. Samuel B. Thomsen, who served at the US embassy in Vientiane as a political officer between 1967 and 1970, recalled: "aid was essentially the infrastructure for the country. Air America and Continental Air Services, the two contract airlines, were the means of communication for the Lao as well as the Americans from north to south".[111]

In a nutshell, Laos's economic and, to a large extent, political structures were shaped by a foreign aid programme that aimed not at economic prosperity of the country but at containing the spread of communism in the region. While the proxy nature of foreign intervention, and an intense conflict in neighbouring Vietnam, made it difficult to properly measure the strength of military and economic capabilities, it could be safely concluded that the level of military and economic capabilities of Laos during neutralisation attempts fell well below the minimum thresholds fixed by our analytical framework.

Summary

Laos was a major failure in the history of application of neutrality as a diplomatic tool for conflict resolution in the international system. While in the previous examples of failure, such as Belgium, Luxemburg, and Norway, neutrality functioned well for over half a century until it was violated by a rising regional hegemon (Germany in 1914), in the case of Laos, almost from the beginning the policy failed to achieve any of its expected aims.

As this analysis indicated, neutralisation may have appeared as a desirable solution to the conflict in Laos; however, apart from its geopolitical location as a buffer nation and its small size, the country did not meet many of the minimum conditions deemed essential for viable permanent neutrality. As observed, due to the asymmetrical, transnational, and ideological nature of the conflict, *the balance of power*, in its conventional definition, was neither achievable nor applicable to the situation in Laos. Similarly, there was no solid consensus among major external stakeholders on the feasibility of neutrality as a long-term solution. The United States saw neutrality as a low-cost, low-profile version of its containment policy in Laos. For the Chinese and the North Vietnamese, neutrality provided a cover and space to consolidate their hold on the country and prepare for the next phase of their political and military manoeuvres.

Also on the domestic side, the country lacked the level of stability, social cohesion, military, and economic capabilities required to uphold neutrality. The persistence of high-level violence, due to deep ethnic and ideological antagonism within the elite, reinforced by external intervention, compounded by strong cross-border tribal and ethnic affiliations, continued to undermine state stability and social cohesion.

A politically divided and poorly skilled Royal Lao Army was incapable of defending neutrality and maintaining law and order. Finally, the country's economy, including the state's budget, was highly dependent on foreign assistance, in the absence of which the Laotian Government was unable to pay the salaries of its officials and soldiers.

Hence, neutrality of Laos failed to meet the five requirements of viable permanent neutrality set forth by our analytical framework. While its geopolitical position—as a small buffer state—fitted the profile of a state suitable for permanent neutrality, it lacked the remaining external and internal determinants of such a state.

The case study of Laos shows the strength of our analytical framework in capturing the main determinants of a viable permanent neutrality; however, a deeper examination of the situation in Laos and in the surrounding region at the time reveals that the failure of Laotian neutrality had more nuances than those explained by our analytical framework. For example, at the time of its neutralisation, Laos was experiencing what Hanggi underlined as "new forms of conflict and warfare which were not covered by the classical notion of neutrality".[112] Hence, insurgency and presence of non-state actors in a conflict added extra constraints on Laos's ability to maintain its neutrality, as well as on the overall application of neutrality-based solutions in future.

Consolidated analysis of the three case studies

The three well-known cases of permanent neutrality were used primarily to illustrate the significance of the external and domestic factors identified in the analytical framework in relation to the viability of permanent neutrality as a conflict management tool and a foreign policy option for small states. The case studies, although quantitatively a small sample, were intended to examine the explanatory power of the proposed analytical framework.

As observed, in the case of Switzerland—the oldest and most often-cited example of permanent neutrality—strong manifestation of domestic determinants of neutrality, such as internal stability and cohesion, and appropriate military and economic capabilities within the Swiss society played a major role in adoption of neutrality as a state policy. However, the absence of understanding and agreement among regional powers on recognition of Swiss neutrality substantially reduced its utility as a viable foreign policy option, as became evident during the Napoleonic conquests in the early nineteenth century. It was only after restoration of a balance of power in Europe and recognition of Switzerland as a permanently neutral state by the participants of the Congress of Vienna in 1815 that the Swiss neutrality encompassed all external and domestic prerequisites of successful permanent neutrality identified by our analytical framework. Ever since, the country managed to maintain her neutrality through thick and thin, including the two World Wars. Over time, building on domestic capabilities and international goodwill, the Swiss further strengthened their utility as a provider of public international good by hosting international organisations and offering offices for mediation. Swiss neutrality evolved into an example of successful foreign policy for small states, as well as a value and character with which the Swiss proudly continue to identify themselves.

Austrian neutrality, on the other hand, emerged as a diplomatic solution for ending the country's occupation and reducing the likelihood of conflict among the great powers. In the early 1950s support for neutrality began to gather momentum among the Austrian political elite. The country's socio-economic and military capabilities to a large extent fit the domestic determinants of viable neutrality. Nonetheless, external players were not ready to recognise Austria's permanent neutrality. Despite the external players' initial intransigencies, Austria's resolve in pushing for consensus among international stakeholders and emergence of an ambience of rapprochement in the post-Stalin policies of the Soviet Union lead to an agreement on independence and permanent neutrality of Austria. Having met all five determinants of a viable permanent neutrality and following Switzerland's step in relation to provision of international public goods, Austria evolved into a successful example of neutrality in the twentieth century.

In the case of Laos, given the situation, neutrality was notionally a highly desirable policy choice. The majority of Lao political elites were conscious of the need for distancing their country from an ensuing ideological conflict in their neighbourhood by adopting a policy of neutrality, which they prematurely did during the first Geneva conference in 1954. Unlike Switzerland and Austria, where strong domestic support and capabilities were followed by international recognition, the prevalence of instability, absence of domestic political consensus, and lack of economic and military capabilities made it partially unfeasible for Laos to uphold and maintain neutrality.

In the early 1960s, an arrangement between the American and Soviet leaders, followed by a rigorous multilateral effort, led to the conclusion of an international agreement on neutralisation of Laos in June 1962. A neutralist-led coalition government backed by an internationally sanctioned neutralisation agreement took Laos closer to meeting most of the prerequisites of a viable neutrality. However, interference by regional players, the trans-border and ideological nature of the conflict, and inadequate domestic capabilities undermined the successful maintenance of neutrality and contributed to the overall failure of the policy in the case of Laos.

The foregoing review of the three case studies clearly demonstrates the strong association between the factors identified in the analytical framework and success in proclamation and maintenance of permanent neutrality.

Equipped with the experiences of the three major permanently neutral states and an empirically tested analytical framework, the next chapter focuses on the historical and conceptual analysis of neutrality in Afghanistan's foreign policy.

Notes

1 Borchert H. Heiko, "Switzerland and Europe's Security Architecture: The Rocky Road from Isolation to Cooperation", eds. E. Reither and H. Gärtner, *Small States and Alliances* (Heidelberg: Physica-Verlag, 2001), pp. 161–182.

2 William D. McCrackan, *The Rise of the Swiss Republic: A History* (New York: H. Holt and Company, 1901), p. 243.

3 Bonjour, *Swiss Neutrality*, p. 16.

4 Ibid, p. 20.

5 Ibid, p. 31.

6 This defensive policy later became known as "Armed Neutrality".

7 Leo Schelbert, *Historical Dictionary of Switzerland* (Lanham, MD: Scarecrow Press, 2007), p. 382.

8 Gordon Sherman, "The Neutrality of Switzerland", *The American Journal of International Law*, 12(2) (April 1918): 245.

9 McCracken, *The Rise of the Swiss Republic*, p. 314.

10 Ibid, p. 316.

11 Bonjour, *Swiss Neutrality*, p. 47.

12 Hofer, *Neutrality as the Principle of Swiss Foreign Policy*, p. 9.

13 Ibid, p. 62.

14 The declaration signed by the great powers on Swiss neutrality in Paris on 20 November 1815 states that "The Powers signatories to the Vienna Declaration

of 20th March hereby formally and authentically recognise the perpetual neutrality of Switzerland and guarantee the integrity and inviolability of her territory within her new boundaries". See Thomas Fischer, "Switzerland: Invention of Permanent Neutrality", ed. Igor S. Novaković, *Neutrality in the 21st Century—Lesson for Serbia* (Belgrad: ISAC Fond, 2013), p. 30.

15 Hofer, *Neutrality as the Principle of Swiss Foreign Policy*, p. 11.

16 Bonjour, *Swiss Neutrality*, p. 54.

17 Ibid, p. 45.

18 Bonjour, *Swiss Neutrality*, p. 99.

19 John F. L. Ross, *Neutrality and International Sanctions: Sweden, Switzerland, and Collective Security* (New York, NY: Praeger, 1989), p. 31.

20 For more information on Germany's desire and attempts to vow Switzerland to their side, please see Bonjour, *Swiss Neutrality*, p. 98.

21 Ibid, p. 108.

22 Georges-Andre Chevallaz, *The Challenge of Neutrality: Diplomacy and the Defence of Switzerland* (Lanham, Maryland: Lexington Books, 2001), p. 3.

23 W. H. McConnell, "The Permanent Neutrality of Austria: 1955–1962" (Masters' Thesis, University of Ottawa, 1962), p. 13.

24 Halbrook notes that invasion called for as many as 500,000 troops; a massive number of men for such a small country. See Stephen Halbrook, *Target Switzerland: Swiss Armed Neutrality in World War II* (New York, NY: Sarpedeon, 1998), p. 137.

25 John Dreyer and Neal G. Jesse, "Swiss Neutrality Examined: Model, Exception or Both?" *Journal of Military and Strategic Studies*, 15(3) (June 2014): 60–83.

26 A report by the US Department of State, May 1997, accuses the Swiss of, among other things, profiteering, collisions with morality, sustaining the Nazi regime, and prolonging the war.

27 John Dreyer and Neal G. Jesse, "Swiss Neutrality Examined: Model, Exception or Both?" *Journal of Military and Strategic Studies* 15(3) (January 2014): 61, 83.

28 McCrackan, *The Rise of the Swiss Republic*, p. 354.

29 Ibid, p. 8.

30 Henry W. Steiger, "The Swiss Army", *The Field Artillery Journal*, 31(8) (1941): 578.

31 The Moscow Conference 1943, "Joint Four Nations Declaration, the section dedicated to Austria, the Foreign Ministers of the US, UK and USSR declared that the annexation (Anschluss) of Austria by Germany was null and void. The declaration called for the establishment of a free Austria after the victory over Nazi Germany".

32 The Swiss Model of neutrality was proposed by Soviets but also contemplated by President Eisenhower and finally agreed to by Austria. Moscow Memorandum 1955 reads "In connection with the conclusion of an Austrian State Treaty to practice a perpetual neutrality of the kind practiced by Switzerland".

33 Herbert Wright, "The Legality of the Annexation of Austria by Germany", *The American Journal of International Law*, 38(4) (October 1944): 633.

34 Article 80 of the Treaty of Versailles states; "Germany acknowledges and will respect strictly the independence of Austria within the frontiers which may be fixed in a Treaty between that State and the Principal Allied and Associated Powers; she agrees that this independence shall be inalienable, except with the consent of the Council of the League of Nations". And article 88 of the Treaty

of St. Germain emphasises that "the independence of Austria is inalienable otherwise than with the consent of the Council of the League of Nations". See Herbert Wright, "The Legality of the Annexation of Austria by Germany", p. 621.

35 Stourzh, "The Origins of Austrian Neutrality", 36.

36 Cronin noted that "within the American bureaucracy there were many who had misgivings about the wisdom of signing a treaty and precipitously ... a bureaucratic struggle ensued between on the one hand those who supported signature of a treaty as the primary objective in seeking a viable Austrian state led by Dean Acheson and his colleagues in the State Department ... and those who supported continued maintenance of the western occupation as the primary means of ensuring a stable, independent Austria led by Secretary of Defence Louis Jahnson". See Audrey Kurth Cronin, "East-West Negotiations over Austria in 1949: Turning-Point in the Cold War", *Journal of Contemporary History*, 24(1) (January 1989): 125–145.

37 Ibid, p. 126.

38 Cronin, "East-West Negotiations over Austria in 1949", p. 125.

39 See Oliver Rathkolb, "The Foreign Relations between the US and Austria in the Late 1950s", eds. Gunter Bischof, Anton Pelinka and Rolf Steininger, *Austria in the Nineteen Fifties* (New Brunswick, NJ: Transaction Publishers, 1995), p. 28.

40 Cronin, "East-West Negotiations over Austria in 1949", p. 149.

41 Cliff Staten, "U.S. Foreign Policy Since World War II: An Essay on Reality's Corrective Qualities" (August 2005).

42 Rathkolb, "The Foreign Relations Between the US and Austria in the Late 1950s", p. 28.

43 Sven Allard, *Russia and the Austrian State Treaty: A Case Study of Soviet Policy in Europe* (University Park, PA: Pennsylvania State University Press, 1970), pp. 109–110.

44 David J. Dallin, *Soviet Foreign Policy After Stalin* (Philadelphia, PA: Lippincott, 1961), p, 145.

45 US Government Printing Office, "Agenda Item 3J The Austrian State Treaty", *Foreign Ministers Meeting; Berlin Discussions*, 25 January to 18 February 1954 (Washington, DC: Superintendent of Documents, 1954), pp. 233–234.

46 Allard, *Russia and the Austrian State Treaty*, p. 116.

47 See Cronin, "East-West Negotiations Over Austria in 1949", p. 144.

48 Audrey Kurth Cronin, *Great Power Politics and the Struggle Over Austria, 1945–1955* (Ithaca, NY: Cornell University Press, 1986), p. 150.

49 Dallin in his book, *Soviet Foreign Policy After Stalin*, refers to 24 October 1955 as the date for withdrawal of last foreign forces from Austria, while Cronin mentions that the last foreign soldiers left Austrian territory on 5 November 1955.

50 Article One of Constitutional Federal Statute (declaration) of Austria's permanent neutrality. See Josef L. Kunz, "Austria's Permanent Neutrality, Reviewed Work", *The American Journal of International Law*, 50(2) (April 1965): 420.

51 Black et al., *Neutralization and World Politics*, 29.

52 Gerard Stourzh, "The Origins of Austrian Neutrality", eds. Nicholas Mercuro and Alan Leonhard, *Neutrality: Changing Concepts and Practices* (New Orleans, LA: University Press of America; Institute for the Comparative Study of Public Policy, University of New Orleans Lanham, 1988), p. 42.

53 Andreas Gémes, "Deconstruction of a Myth? Austria and the Hungarian Refugees of 1956–57", eds. S. Dempsey and D. Nichols, *Time, Memory, and Cultural Change* (Vienna: IWM Junior Visiting Fellows' Conferences, 2009).

54 Vienna hosted a US-Soviet leaders summit in 1961. Austria also played an important role in easing tension during the Cuban missile crisis of 1962. See Oliver Rathkolb, "Bruno Kreisky: Perspectives of Top Level US Foreign Policy Decision Makers, 1959–1983", *Contemporary Austrian Studies*, 2 (1994): 132–133.

55 Andras Kovacs and Ruth Wodak eds, *NATO, Neutrality and National Identity: The Case of Austria and Hungary* (Vienna: Böhlau Verlag Ges. m. b. H. & Co. Köln·Weimar, 2003), p. 13.

56 The American's calculation was that, since German and Italian borders with Austria were defensible in the case of a possible Soviet attack, full military control of Austria could only provide a buffer zone for slowing Soviet invasion. Hence a forward defence of Austria was not strategically vital for NATO's defence policy and a neutral but sympathetic Austria would better serve the purpose. See James Jay Carafano, *Waltzing Into the Cold War: The Struggle for Occupied Austria* (College Station, Texas: Texas A&M University Press, 2002), p. 153.

57 Cronin, *Great Power Politics and the Struggle Over Austria*, p. 156.

58 Stourzh, "The Origins of Austrian Neutrality", p. 45.

59 Ibid, p. 45.

60 Wolfgang Mueller, "Peaceful Coexistence, Neutrality, and Bilateral Relations across the Iron Curtain: Introduction", eds. Arnold Suppan and Wolfgang Mueller, *Peaceful Coexistence or Iron Curtain Austria, Neutrality, and Eastern Europe in the Cold War and Detente, 1955–1989* (Vienna: LIT, 2009), p. 12.

61 Stourzh, "The Origins of Austrian Neutrality", p. 42.

62 The Indian Government through its Ambassador in Moscow, acting as intermediary for the Austrians, went further and suggested permanent neutrality as the basis for a treaty. See "The 1955 State Treaty and Austrian Neutrality". Available at: http://countrystudies.us/austria/47.htm.

63 "Drastic Food Rationing in the Ruhr", *The Canberra Times*, 7 May 1947.

64 From 1947 to 1953 Austria received economic aid in the amount of roughly US$1.1 billion. See Josef Haas, "60 Years of Marshall Plan Aid—A Critical Appraisal from an Austrian Perspective".

65 Maddison historical data. Available at: http://worldeconomics.com/Data/Madison HistoricalGDP/Madison%20Historical%20GDP%20Data.efp.

66 Oliver Rathkolb, "International Perceptions of Austrian Neutrality post 1945", eds. Gunter Bischof, Anton Pelinka, and Ruth Wodak, "Neutrality in Austria", *Contemporary Austria Studies*, Volume 9 (New Brunswick, NJ: Transaction Publishers, 2001), p. 3.

67 Rathkolb, "The Foreign Relations between the US and Austria in the Late 1950s", p. 30.

68 Oliver Rathkolb, "International Perceptions of Austrian Neutrality Post 1945", p. 11.

69 Cronin, *Great Power Politics and the Struggle over Austria, 1945–1955*, p. 168.

70 Withdrawal of Soviet support and the subsequent resolution of the Austrian-Yugoslav dispute over the territory of Carinthia removed a technical obstacle in the process of neutralisation of Austria. In another example, permanent neutrality according to Edmund Herzig, the absence of irredentist claims by Turkmenistan

despite a sizeable Turkmen minority in Iran, has made its unilateral declaration of permanent neutrality more credible. See Edmund Herzig, "Iran and Central Asia", eds. Roy Allison and Lena Jonson, *Central Asian Security. The New International Context* (Washington, DC: Brookings Institution, 2001), p. 184.

71 Black argues that the main objective of neutralisation of Laos in 1962 was to moderate conflict in Laos not to prevent international conflict or settlement of broader issues in South East Asia. See Black et al., *Neutralization and World Politics*, p. 4.

72 Heiner Hanggi, "ASEAN and the ZOPFAN Concept", Regional Strategic Studies Program, Institute of Southeast Asian Studies (Singapore: 1991), p. 9.

73 Martin Stuart-Fox, *A History of Laos* (New York, NY: Cambridge University Press Cambridge, 1997), p. 6.

74 Hugh Toye, *Laos: Buffer State or Battleground* (London and New York, NY: Oxford University Press, 1968), p. 65.

75 Arthur J. Dommen, *Conflict in Laos: The Politics of Neutralization* (London: Pall Mall Press, 1964), p. 22.

76 Dommen, *Conflict in Laos: The Politics of Neutralization*, p. 38.

77 The final Declaration of the Geneva Conference on the Problem of restoring peace in Indochina, 21 July 1954. In Dommen, *Conflict in Laos: The Politics of Neutralization*, p. 307.

78 Declaration by the Royal Government of Laos, 21 July 1954. In Dommen, *Conflict in Laos: The Politics of Neutralization*, p. 308.

79 Stuart-Fox, *A History of Laos*, p. 94.

80 Dommen, *Conflict in Laos: The Politics of Neutralization*, p. 99.

81 Ibid, p. 167.

82 Roland A. Paul, "Laos: Anatomy of an American Involvement", *Foreign Affairs*, 49(3) (April 1971): 533–547.

83 Stuart-Fox, *A History of Laos*, p. 118.

84 On 23 March, President Kennedy appeared on nationwide television to read a statement on Laos. See Foreign Relations, 1961–1963, Volume XXIV, and Laos Crisis. Office of the Historian Documents 39–58.

85 Jürg Martin Gabriel, "Neutrality and Neutralism in Southeast Asia, 1960–1970", *Eidgenössische Technische Hochschule, Forschungsstelle für Internationale Beziehungen*, 9 (2002): 9.

86 Ibid, p. 219.

87 Treaty Series No. 27 (1963), the Declaration and Protocol on the Neutrality of Laos, Geneva, 23 July 1963 (London: HMSO, May 1963).

88 Treaty Series No. 27 (1963), the Declaration and Protocol on the Neutrality of Laos, Geneva, 23 July 1963, Cmnd, 2025 (London: HMSO, May, 1963).

89 Roland A. Paul, "Laos: Anatomy of an American Involvement", *Foreign Affairs*, 49(3) (April 1971): 533.

90 For more details about the incident, see P. F. Langer and J. J. Zasloff, "Revolution in Laos: The North Vietnamese and the Pathet Lao", RM-5935, RAND Corporation (September 1969), p. 113.

91 Stuart-Fox uses a more native pronunciation of names rather than their anglicised versions.

92 Stuart-Fox, *A History of Laos*, p. 125.

93 Arthur J. Dommen, *Conflict in Laos: The Politics of Neutralization*, p. 221.

94 From late 1963 to 1973 the CIA was engaged in a covert war against the Pathet Lao and North Vietnamese forces inside Laos. For more information of on the

"Secret War", see James E. Parker, *Covert Ops: The CIA's Secret War in Laos* (New York, NY: St. Martin's Paperbacks, 1997).
95 See Secret War in Laos. Available at: http://legaciesofwar.org/about-laos/secret -war-laos/.
96 Stuart-Fox, *A History of Laos*, p. 136.
97 Anoulak Kittikhoun, "Small State, Big Revolution: Geography and the Revolution in Laos", *Theory and Society*, 38(1) (January 2009): 25–55.
98 See Toye, *Laos: Buffer State or Battleground.*
99 Gabriel, *Neutrality and Neutralism in Southeast Asia, 1960–1970*, p. 5.
100 Anoulak Kittikhoun argued that "the historical rivalry between Thailand and Vietnam also turned out to reflect the conflicts played out over Laos during the revolution". See Anoulak Kittikhoun, "Small State, Big Revolution: Geography and the Revolution in Laos", *Theory and Society*, 38(1) (January 2009): 25–55.
101 Arthur argued that the majority of the signatories of the international agreement on neutrality of Laos were doubtful about the viability of the deal. The Chinese, and their allies in particular, considered the deal a step toward the full liberation of Laos from Western influence. Also see Dommen, *Conflict in Laos: The Politics of Neutralization*, p. 221.
102 Kittikhoun, "Small State, Big Revolution", p. 26.
103 Toye, *Laos: Buffer State or Battleground*, p. 104.
104 Hanggi, *ASEAN and the ZOPFAN Concept*, p. 9.
105 Dommen, *Conflict in Laos: The Politics of Neutralization*, p. 292.
106 Toye, *Laos: Buffer State or Battleground*, p. 110.
107 Bernard B. Fall, "Reappraisal in Laos", *Current History* 42 (January, 1962): 9.
108 "Hearings II: Committee on Government Operation, House of Representatives. United States Aid Operations in Laos: Seventh Report by the Committee. June 15, 1959 (86th Cong., 1st sess.)" (Washington, DC: Government Printing Office, 1959).
109 Viliam Phraxayavong and University of Sydney. School of Geosciences, *History of Aid to Laos: Motivations and Impacts* (Chiang Mai, Thailand: Mekong Press, 2007), p. 1.
110 Statistics and Reports Division, US Foreign Assistance and Assistance from International Organizations—Obligations and Loan Authorizations (Washington: 1964), quoted in Dommen, *Conflict in Laos: The Politics of Neutralization*, p. 105.
111 The Association for Diplomatic Studies and Training, Laos Country Readers. Interview with Samuel B. Thomsen, Political Officer at the US embassy from 1967–1970, 10.
112 Hanggi, *ASEAN and the ZOPFAN Concept*, p. 12.

4 Neutrality in Afghanistan's foreign policy

The roots of Afghanistan's policy of neutrality/*bitarafi* can be traced back to its nineteenth-century buffer status and an isolationist stand aimed at avoiding aggression from its large hostile neighbours. Hence, examination of Afghanistan's policy of neutrality would be incomplete without comprehending the country's role as a buffer state[1] between rival British and Russian, later Soviet, imperial forces in the nineteenth and early twentieth centuries.

From the 1870s, when Anglo-Russian relations witnessed a better rapport, the two empires began to settle their differences over the control of Central Asia and came to an understanding: to accept Afghanistan as a buffer state where neither power would seek to increase its influence to the detriment of the other. Afghanistan effectively remained a buffer state from the late nineteenth century until the British pulled out of the region in 1947.

Afghanistan as a buffer state

Afghanistan is a classic case in the study of buffer systems in the context of international politics. The term buffer state, according to Thomas Ross,[2] was first used in 1883 by British India officials in reference to Afghanistan. Ludwig Adamec, an expert on Afghanistan's diplomatic history, calls the period of 1880–1919 "the period of defensive isolationism and buffer-state politics".[3] Turning Afghanistan into a buffer state stemmed from Britain's India defence policy, with the aim of containing Russia's expansion beyond Central Asia and Persia, while at the same time avoiding a direct confrontation with Russian forces in the region. In the early nineteenth century senior British India officers were of the belief that the native people living beyond India's northwest frontiers would not be an existential threat to their holdings unless assisted by or allied with European powers.[4] Thus, the nature of British policy in Afghanistan depended on the level of threat perceived to be caused by the interference of a European power—in this case, Russia.

According to Vartan Gregorian, "[t]his policy called for an accelerated con-solidation of British power in India and an extension of British political influence in nearby countries".[5]

Russia, on the other hand, knew that it could not put effective pressure on Britain except in Afghanistan, and sought to draw maximum advantage from British vulnerability in the subcontinent. Tsar Nicholas II once proudly wrote to his sister,

> it is pleasant for me to know that I and *only* I possess the ultimate means of deciding the course of the war in South Africa. It is very simple—just a telegraphic order to all the troops in Turkestan to mobilise and advance toward the Indian frontier. Not even the strongest fleet in the world can keep us from striking England at this, her most vulnerable point.[6]

However, after rounds of failed military campaigns by the British, and futile attempts by the Russians to win over fugitive and incumbent Afghan Amirs and princes, both imperial powers reached a tacit agreement accepting Afghanistan as a buffer state and employed a clever combination of diplo-macy and coercion to enforce Afghanistan's buffer status.

The Anglo-Russian "Granville-Gorchakov" agreement of 1873, which delimited the north-eastern frontiers of Afghanistan and Russian protec-torates in Central Asia by annexing the Wakhan Corridor to the territory of Afghanistan, was the initial step toward formalisation of a buffer zone between the two imperial powers.[7]

The next stage in turning Afghanistan from a nominal into a real buffer state came in 1893, when Amir Abdul Rahman apparently consented to British India foreign secretary Sir Mortimer Durand's proposed delinea-tion of eastern and southern boundaries of his dominions, and the North-West Frontiers of India. However, despite these developments, there was only an informal understanding between the British and Russian empires about Afghanistan's buffer status. Russia was eager to have a commercial presence and direct lines of communication with the Amir of Afghanistan, which was not uncommon in a buffer system. However, for British India officials, Russia's economic primacy in Central Asia and Persia, its close relationship with the Shah of Persia, and attempts to open direct channels of communication with the Amir of Afghanistan were viewed as sources of serious threat to India's security. As part of the Anglo-Russia entente of the early twentieth century, the two powers finally concluded a convention in 1907 on the status of Persia, Afghanistan, and Tibet. The convention recog-nised that Afghanistan falls within the British sphere of influence, with all diplomatic and foreign communication with the Kingdom of Afghanistan to be conducted via British intermediaries. The Anglo-Russian Convention was the final step in the transformation of Afghanistan into a buffer, and from 1907 onwards Afghanistan became an officially recognised buffer state and effectively[8] remained a buffer state from the late nineteenth century until the British pulled out of the region in 1947.

From a regional security perspective, Afghanistan's positioning as a buffer state was arguably an effective instrument for maintaining the balance of power in the region for almost a hundred years.[9] It appears that the buffer state status also served the domestic interests of the Afghan Amirs, as they received substantial amounts of cash and arms from the British and some assistance from the Russians while hoping to avoid direct influence of the British and Russians in their internal affairs. The policy of neutrality, albeit in its negative connotation, "isolation" from the infidel's influence, was also favoured by Afghanistan's religious, tribal, and ethnic leaders.[10]

Neutrality in Afghanistan's foreign policy

When Afghanistan found itself caught in the middle of a great power struggle for dominance in the region and subsequently reduced to a buffer state between the rival British and Russian empires, neutrality was seen as a rational foreign policy choice to ensure its sovereignty and survival. However, striking a correct balance whilst upholding and sustaining neutrality was a task full of challenges.

The first instance of Afghanistan upholding a policy of neutrality with some degree of independence occurred during the First World War. Though supposedly still a British protectorate and proscribed from making its own foreign policy, Afghanistan faced the real choice of entering the war or remaining neutral. Domestically, the decision to remain neutral became particularly challenging when in late October in 1914, the Ottoman Empire, the de facto leader of the Islamic world, joined the war in support of the Central Powers against Britain.

Britain and Russia urged the Afghan ruler, Amir Habibullah I (1901–1919), to avoid the disaster of a world war by remaining neutral. In September 1914, King George V sent a letter to Habibullah reminding him that neutrality was in the interest of Afghanistan, urging him to remain neutral, and finally assuring him of an eventual British and allied victory.[11]

Habibullah initially declared Afghanistan a neutral country,[12] but subsequent developments seriously tested the Amir's ability to uphold this policy. In September 1915 a Turco-German delegation known as the "Niedermayer-Hentig Expedition" arrived in Kabul to attempt to persuade Habibullah to help the Central Powers. At the same time, certain members of the ruling family led by Nasrullah Khan (the Amir's brother) and a pan-Islamist Afghan intelligentsia led by Mahmud Tarzi (editor-in-chief of the only Afghan newspaper, *Siraj al-Akhbar*) were also lobbying in favour of an alliance with the Turks and Germans.[13]

British authorities in India demanded that, as a neutral country, Afghanistan should arrest and disarm the members of the Niedermayer-Hentig delegation, who represented belligerent states. Habibullah didn't consider the delegation's visit to Afghanistan a breach of neutrality. Instead he entertained the Turco-German delegation for nearly two years without giving them a definite response. Similarly, he waited 16 months before replying to King George's letter, in January 1916.

Habibullah took his time to examine the course of the war. He tried to strengthen domestic support for his policy of neutrality by holding a consultative gathering/*Jirga*, in October 1915.[14] A week after replying to King George's letter and reiterating his commitment to neutrality, he signed a treaty of friendship with Germany. The treaty was more of a tactical step to appease the pro-German domestic lobby and provide a face-saving exit for the Niedermayer-Hentig delegation rather than a serious commitment to joining the war against British interests in India. Immediately after signing the treaty, Habibullah privately reassured the British envoy of his resolve to uphold Afghanistan's neutrality. By signing the treaty with Germany, the Amir also wanted to send a signal to the British that he was determined to act as an independent sovereign.

With hindsight, one can argue that neutrality was the most rational policy for Afghanistan at the time, and one that enabled Habibullah to secure promises of concessions from the British and a treaty of friendship with Germany.

After the conclusion of the war, it became apparent that the size of British concessions neither matched Kabul's aspiration for independence nor corresponded with the difficulties the Amir had endured to confine domestic dissatisfaction with his policy, and prevent the uprising of the frontier tribes against British India.[15] The nationalists were emboldened and Habibullah lost the remaining support he enjoyed during the war (he was subsequently assassinated in February of 1919).

From a conceptual and international legal viewpoint, this first episode of Afghanistan's neutrality fits the general definition of wartime neutrality as described in the 1907 Hague Convention.[16] Given the above-mentioned setbacks, the wartime practice of neutrality did not transform into a peacetime policy of neutrality.

Independent foreign policy and the search for allies

After ascending the throne in Kabul, the reformist Afghan King Amanullah (1919–1929), son of Habibullah, in his first formal correspondence with the

British pressed for negotiations that would grant Afghanistan full independence. Britain's rejection of the demand prompted Amanullah to unilaterally declare Afghanistan an independent country on 19 April 1919.[17]

Contrary to his father's defensive policies, Amanullah initiated a political and diplomatic offensive to compel Britain to recognise Afghanistan's independence. He ended Afghanistan's policy of isolation, appointed Mahmud Tarzi as the first Foreign Minister, and dispatched Mohammad Wali Khan Darwazi as his first Ambassador-at-large to negotiate the establishment of diplomatic relations with countries around the world.[18] Between 1919 and 1922, Afghanistan signed treaties of bilateral cooperation with Russia, Turkey, France, Italy, and Iran.[19] In search of new alliances, Darwazi travelled to Washington, D.C., in July 1921. He met with President Warren G. Harding, solicited diplomatic recognition and asked for the establishment of economic ties between Afghanistan and the United States. The US Government, which considered Afghanistan as part of the British sphere of influence, declined to confer diplomatic recognition or invest in Afghanistan.

Amanullah's ambitious attempt to attract new allies, and his closer ties with Soviet Russia, which provided generous financial and technical support, did not end Afghanistan's economic and military dependence on British India. He failed to realise that even as a fully independent country recognised by a dozen regional and European nations, striking a "correct balance" in relations with the British and Soviet empires would have to remain the fundamental principle of Afghanistan's foreign policy. Abdul Samad Ghaus, author and former Deputy Foreign Minister (1973–1978), even suggests that Amanullah's unorthodox foreign policy—hostile toward Britain while welcoming Russians and other Europeans—may have contributed to the collapse of his rule in 1929, when he was deposed following tribal uprisings.[20]

Return to neutrality and keeping the balance

After the brief stint of Amir Habibullah Kalakani, the leader of the uprising that deposed Amanullah, Mohammed Nadir, a former military chief, seized power in Kabul. Nadir Shah (1929–1933) favoured closer ties with Britain, which had supported him in his campaign for power. According to Ghaus, "Nadir Shah saw to it that the Afghan foreign policy, having wandered from its natural course, was brought back into line … The pendulum, which had gone too far to the left, swung back to the middle".[21]

Nadir, in his opening remarks to the opening session of the Afghan National Assembly, stated, "The best and most fruitful policy that one can imagine for Afghanistan is a policy of neutrality. Afghanistan must give its neighbours assurances of its friendly attitudes while safeguarding the right of reciprocity".[22] While at the official level Nadir Shah elevated neutrality as the core principle of Afghanistan's foreign policy, the most significant challenge he faced, according to the historian Vartan Gregorian, was "to make Afghan neutrality a reality and to convince all elements, including the Soviets and the Muslim nationalist-modernists inside and outside the country, that he was not a tool of British imperialism".[23]

Nadir took a series of steps to build confidence in his policy of neutrality. He re-affirmed the past Anglo-Afghan treaties and signed a new treaty of neutrality and non-aggression with the Soviet Union.[24] To further convince his powerful neighbours that Afghanistan would be truly neutral, Nadir did not take sides in subsequent conflicts and Pashtun uprisings against British India in tribal areas, refrained from intervening in the affairs of Soviet Central Asia, and expelled Central Asian independence fighters from northern Afghanistan. He struck the "correct balance" in his ties with Britain and the Soviet Union, avoiding them as much as possible, and increasingly engaged with the "third powers", such as Germany, France, and Italy, in the development of economic and education sectors.

Nadir's reign came to an abrupt end with his assassination in November 1933. The delicate tasks of maintaining balance in foreign policy and nurturing his peacetime policy of neutrality were left to his teenage successor, Mohammed Zahir, and his conservative younger brother, Mohamed Hashim, who served as regent. While the young king remained the *de jure* sovereign, Hashim actually steered Afghanistan's foreign relations over the next 13 years.

Zahir did not make direct reference to Afghanistan's neutrality in his first major policy speech to the parliament in 1934. Instead, he alluded to a unilateral policy of non-aggression *vis-à-vis* neighbours and in return expected reciprocal treatment from other nations. Gregorian argues that "in practice the Hashim government was guided by the same principles as Nadir in foreign policy".[25] However, there are instances, such as Afghanistan's participation in the Saadabad Pact of 1937—a regional security alliance[26] allegedly aimed at containing Soviet influence, and Kabul's growing political and economic ties with Nazi Germany—that indicate an increasing desire for forging alliances as and when such opportunities were available.

Back to strict wartime neutrality

Once again anxious of provoking either of its powerful neighbours, Afghanistan found it imperative not to take part in the Second World War. On 6 September 1939, Zahir Shah, on the advice of his prime minister (and uncle) Mohammad Hashim, declared that Afghanistan would not join any of the warring alliances and would remain neutral.[27] Much like the episode of neutrality during the

First World War, during the Second World War the Hashim government faced serious pressure from within the government ranks from three prominent sources. First, an active and strong ultranationalist and somewhat pro-German constituency existed at the highest ranks of government, including two of his favourite nephews (Zahir Shah's cousins) Prince Daud and Naim, who later became the Prime Minister and the Foreign Minister, respectively. Second, the presence of nearly two hundred German and Italian technical experts inside Afghanistan, some of whom were accused of subversive activities[28] against British interests in the tribal areas. And third, Germany's generous investment in nascent economic and financial sectors[29] and a general public sympathy for Germany in contrast to a popular suspicion and disgust toward British and Soviet activities in the country. However, Zahir Shah's declaration of neutrality had the support of his powerful prime minister, who, according to Siddiq Farhang, a former top bureaucrat for the late king, "had the final say on all policy matters".[30] To strengthen their position, the King called a grand assembly of elders (*Loya Jirga*), held in November 1941, to deliberate on the policy of neutrality and provide advice on the allies' demands for the eviction of all suspicious Axis nationals from Afghan territory.[31]

The *Jirga* overwhelmingly supported the government's policy of neutrality and announced that Afghanistan would not allow belligerents to use its territory against each other, and that the country stood ready to defend itself against foreign aggression. The *Jirga* also recommended that the German and Italian nationals be given a dignified and safe exit to their home countries.[32] Except for a small number of diplomats that remained in Kabul, the rest of the Axis nationals were deported from Afghanistan to Turkey under the guarantee of safe passage.

With a few exceptions, as previously noted, during the period from 1930 to 1945, Afghanistan pursued an internationally sanctioned policy of wartime neutrality, and a peacetime neutrality very similar to the policies followed by other neutral states at the time.[33] However, rapid and dramatic shifts in post-war international and regional contexts—such as the demise of the British Empire, the emergence of the Soviet Union and the United States as the two dominant global powers with competing ideologies, and most crucially, the creation of Pakistan as an independent state encompassing the frontier Pashtun tribes—forced the Afghan Government to review its foreign and domestic policies. While the older and more conservative policymakers, such as Hashim, thought that Afghanistan could continue its buffer-neutral state policy by replacing the British with the Americans in the traditional balancing formula, the younger and more hard-line group—the troika of Daud, Naim, and Majid Zabuli, an industrialist and later Minister of National Economy—began to demand radical reforms in foreign and domestic policies.

Badly bruised by post-partition developments, including the lack of international sympathy for Afghanistan's position on the issue of the Durand Line, which demarcated the border between Afghanistan and Pakistan,[34] and the ultimate incorporation of the Pashtun tribal areas east of the Durand Line into the newly established state of Pakistan, King Zahir was forced to adopt a harder line. While the period under the prime ministership of Shah Mahmoud (1946–1953) saw some improvement in relations with the outside world (particularly with the United States),[35] Zahir's appointment of his cousin, Mohammed Daud, effectively marked the end of Afghanistan's long held tradition of neutrality.

The policies followed by successive Afghan governments, first by Daud and later through the Soviet occupation, could be described as "neutralism", "positive neutrality", and "non-alignment", differing in meaning and scope from the way that Afghanistan had previously interpreted its policy of neutrality. While Afghanistan had maintained a certain balance in its foreign policy until the Soviet invasion in 1979, any discussion on Afghanistan's neutrality beyond this period, particularly from the 1955 Bandung Conference that created the Non-aligned Movement, needs to consider this shift in the concept and practice of neutrality.[36]

From neutrality to neutralism and non-alignment

Prime Minister Daud (1953–1963) quickly embarked on a reform and modernisation drive which, according to Saikal, pivoted on "three interrelated policy goals: to centralise power as comprehensively as possible under his leadership; to institute a command-based process of speedy social and economic change; and to promote Pashtunism as the foundation for Afghan nationalism".[37]

To achieve these goals, Daud introduced revolutionary changes in the structure of his cabinet. First, he appointed a group of like-minded young and highly educated ministers. He was acutely aware that his goals could not be realised without economic, military, and political support from external sources. Strict adherence to traditional (passive) neutrality limited his ability to enlist much-needed foreign assistance in pursuit of his domestic and regional ambitions.

Daud calculated that a shift in foreign policy was possible since the strategic imperatives that had forced Afghanistan to be a buffer-neutral state in the past had disappeared. With the British departure from India, Afghanistan was no longer constrained by keeping the "correct balance" between its northern and southern neighbours. During this period, Afghanistan was actively engaged in a territorial and political dispute with Pakistan and was eagerly looking for partners to strengthen its own position.

Hence, Daud redefined neutrality in a way that enabled him to attract military and political support from the Soviet Union in particular. Explaining this shift in the government's outlook toward neutrality, Sayed Qasim Reshtia, author and Press Minister in the 1960s, affirms that while in the past Afghanistan followed a policy of passive neutrality, mainly to appease its powerful neighbours, the new government employed a positive and active type of neutrality which "was based on the national interest and independent judgement of the people of Afghanistan".[38] This new policy, according to Abdul Rahman Pazhwak, Afghanistan's permanent representative at the United Nations in the 1960s, was intended to preserve close and friendly relations with the United States and the USSR, and receive unconditional assistance while not being forced to align with either side.[39] Reshtia argues that in the early years the adoption of this policy enabled Afghanistan to receive a considerable amount of development aid from various sources, including from the US Government.[40]

Over time, frustrated by America's lack of interest in meaningful assistance and Washington's pro-Pakistani approach,[41] Daud found the Soviet bloc was a more responsive partner. Politically, he joined the Non-aligned Movement to maintain a veneer of Afghanistan's neutral posture and preserve his ability to engage all sides. From this point, in the words of Reshtia, "Afghanistan's neutrality had evolved into active nonalignment".[42]

On the 17 July 1973, Daud (now the Afghan President after a bloodless coup against Zahir Shah), described this new form of neutrality in a national address:

> The foreign policy of Afghanistan is based on neutrality, non-participation in military pacts, and independent judgment of the issues by the people themselves. Emanating from our national aspirations, this policy is designed to fulfil the material and spiritual needs of the people.[43]

By this time, however, and according to William Piez, an economic and political officer at the US embassy (1963–1966), Afghanistan was:

> Considered to be a neutral country but with a pretty strong Communist influence. Their [Afghanistan's] representative at the UN almost always voted on the Soviet side of any issue and was recognised by American political analysts as essentially a kind of stalking horse for the Russians whenever an important issue came up.[44]

Perhaps neither President Daud nor other Afghan policymakers and intellectuals of the time foresaw the historical outcome: that President Daud's emotional and obsessive Pakistan-centric foreign and security policy drove

Afghanistan deeply into the Soviet orbit. The so-called "unconditional" assistance and training offered by the Eastern bloc brought with it a zealous ideology which soon pervaded all levels of Afghan Government and society and sowed the seeds of instability and destruction for decades to come.

The Soviet invasion of Afghanistan ended what was left of its autonomy and policy of neutrality, although the Soviet-backed regimes would continue to espouse neutrality in their rhetoric. Even within the NAM, the invasion caused a serious division between members when Yugoslavia and some Arab states decided to condemn it on the basis of NAM's principle of non-interference. The effort was promptly suppressed by a joint Soviet and Cuban diplomatic offensive.[45]

Ironically, even the Afghan communist regimes, despite their obvious military dependence and ideological association with the Soviet Union, formally remained committed to the rhetoric of neutrality. Prime Minister Noor Mohammed Taraki, in a radio address in May 1978, avowed that "the Democratic Republic of Afghanistan adheres to a policy of non-alignment and positive and active neutrality … based on principles of peaceful coexistence".[46]

Afghanistan officially remained a member of NAM after the 1989 Soviet withdrawal and the fall of the last communist regime in 1992, as well as during the five troubled years of the Mujahideen government in Kabul from 1992 to 1996. Given that this was a period of civil war, with a badly divided government, there was no real possibility of making an independent foreign policy. The Taliban regime that followed (1996–2001) was more of an ideological movement than a government with articulated domestic and foreign policy goals. As Olivier Roy once emphasised, "The Taliban have no foreign policy".[47] Moreover, the Taliban regime was not recognised by the wider international community,[48] and no records were found to indicate their official position *vis-à-vis* Afghanistan's neutrality and membership in NAM.

Attitude toward neutrality during Hamid Karzai presidency

The post-2001 government of Afghanistan remained an active member of the NAM and regularly participated in the movement's meetings. However, it has refrained from using the term *neutrality* in its official statements. While most previous Afghan leaders considered neutrality as a principle of Afghan foreign policy, at least rhetorically, President Karzai was particularly sensitive about even references to neutrality.[49] On a number of occasions he openly discussed the desire to strengthen ties between Afghanistan and NATO member states.

In interviews conducted during the course of research for a paper on the history of neutrality in Afghanistan's foreign policy,[50] some senior cabinet members went further, challenging the whole logic of Afghanistan's traditional neutrality and disagreeing with the proposition that neutrality was the most suitable foreign policy for Afghanistan. Instead, recalling the Russian invasion of 1979, these ministers argued that Afghanistan's neutrality, especially in the absence of a credible domestic or international enforcement mechanism, made the country vulnerable to foreign aggression. One of the ministers added emphatically that, had Afghanistan joined the Western-led alliances of the time, such as SEATO and Central Treaty Organisation (CENTO), and had Afghanistan maintained a more strategic, not Pakistan-centric, attitude toward its relationship with the United States, the Soviet leadership would have thought twice before invading the country in 1979.[51]

Summary

Historically, neutrality/*bitarafi* has been a prominent feature of Afghanistan's foreign policy; however, very little is known about the nature and the latitude of this policy. Given the constant changes in the nature of Afghan neutrality, it is equally difficult to describe, based on the literature available, what specific type of neutrality, if at all, Afghanistan has pursued in the past. Nevertheless, this study can offer three broad conclusions. First, Afghanistan's post-independence policy of neutrality was not a strategic choice crafted through a usual policymaking process but a meek continuation of a colonially imposed buffer policy. Second, despite some consistency in official statements of the various Afghan governments regarding Afghanistan's buffer-neutral status, in practice, except during the two World Wars, Afghanistan was never a truly neutral state. The Afghan rulers, as argued by Louis Dupree, from time to time used a broad and loose definition of the concept of neutrality that is *bitarafi*, often for their own convenience. Over time, Afghanistan's traditional neutrality/*bitarafi* evolved into positive neutrality, neutralism, and non-alignment. Three, the policy of neutrality often acted as a fall-back position to which the Afghan rulers could return whenever other alternatives failed.

Hence, this historical analysis of neutrality in Afghanistan's foreign policy does not support the argument used by the proponents of neutrality, namely, that Afghanistan was a neutral state in the past and therefore it is amenable to becoming a permanently neutral state in the future. However, the historical analysis does not offer a definitive answer to the question of the feasibility and desirability of permanent neutrality as a long-term policy choice for Afghanistan. A comprehensive analysis of feasibility and desirability is offered in the final chapter.

Notes

1 Afghanistan's role as buffer, later neutral, state could also be examined with the help of a role approach in foreign policy. Afghanistan did not chose, but was compelled, to become a buffer and later a neutral state due to geography and international system requirements. See Sofiane Sekhri, "The Role Approach as a Theoretical Framework for the Analysis of Foreign Policy in Third World Countries", *African Journal of Political Science and International Relations*, 3(10) (October 2009): 423–432.

2 Ross, "Buffer States: A Geographic's Perspective", p. 16.

3 Ludwig W. Adamec, *Historical Dictionary of Afghanistan* (NJ and London: Scarecrow Press, 1991), p. 15.

4 Richard Colley Wellesley and Robert Montgomery Martin eds., *The Despatches, Minutes, and Correspondence of the Marquess Wellesley, K. G., During His Administration in India—5 Volume Set* (1837), p. 173.

5 Vartan Gregorian, *The Emergence of Modern Afghanistan* (Stanford, Calif: Stanford University Press, 1969), p. 92.

6 Apollon Davidson, "Russia and South Africa Before the Soviet Era", *Working Papers, National Research University, Higher School of Economics* (2013).

7 The establishment of a Wakhan Corridor and annexing it to the Afghan state by the "Granville-Gorchakov" agreement of 1873 was designed to create as narrow an Afghan buffer zone between British India and Russian Central Asia. See Kamoludin Abdullaev and Shahram Akbarzadeh, *Historical Dictionary of Tajikistan* (Lanham, Maryland: Scarecrow Press, April 2010); 2nd edition, p. 91.

8 Theoretically, it could be argued that the demise of the Tsarist regime in Russia and Afghanistan's proclamation of independence in 1919 changed the country's role as a buffer state between the two imperial powers; however, in practice Afghanistan remained a buffer zone until British departure from the subcontinent in 1947.

9 On 31 August 1907, a convention was signed between Great Britain and Russia formalising the arrangements on the Subject of Persia, Afghanistan, and Tibet. The text of the Convention is available at "Convention Signed on August 31, 1907, between Great Britain and Russia, Containing Arrangements on the Subject of Persia, Afghanistan and Tibet", *The American Journal of International Law*, 1(4) (October 1907): 398–406.

10 Afghan Amirs under the influence of religious and tribal leaders resisted the presence of foreign officers inside Afghanistan; for example in 1869, one of the major concessions Shir Ali Khan received from Lord Mayo was the promise that "no European officers would be placed as Resident in his cities". See Sir Owen Tudor Burne, "British Agents in Afghanistan", *Books in English*, Paper 12 (London: W. H. Allen and Co., 1879). Digitised Afghanistan Materials in English from the Arthur Paul Afghanistan Collection.

11 A copy of the letter from King George V to His Majesty, the Amir of Afghanistan is printed as an appendix on page 205 of Ludwig W. Adamec's, *Afghanistan 1900–1923: A Diplomatic History* (Santa Barbara, CA: University of California Press, 1967), p. 205.

12 Editorial of *Siraj al-Akhbar*, 21 October, 1914, p. 1, reported Amir's proclamation of neutrality. Name of the author is not mentioned; however, it is assumed to be Mahmoud Baig Tarzi, the editor-in-chief of the newspaper.

13 Ludwig W. Adamec, *Afghanistan's Foreign Affairs to the Mid-Twentieth Century: Relations with the USSR, Germany, and Britain* (Tucson, Ariz: University of Arizona Press, 1974), p. 27.

14 Buchholz (2007) and Hanifi (2004), argue that while the history of Jirgas in Afghanistan goes back centuries, the traditional Afghan elder's consultative gathering was officially called "Loya Jirga" in 1923. See Loya jirga-i 'umumi dar Jalalabad (1923, March 16), *Aman-i Afghan*, pp. 11–12 and Benjamin Buchholz, "Thoughts on Afghanistan's Loya Jirga: A Myth?" *Asien*, 104 (July 2007): 27.

15 British India authorities apparently promised Amir Habibullah that if he maintained Afghanistan's neutrality and cooperated with them, the British Government would grant Afghanistan full independence once the war ended; however, he was offered only some weapons and cash. See Abdul Samad Ghaus, *The Fall of Afghanistan: An Insider's Account* (Oxford: Brassey, 1988), p. 25.

16 The full text of the Convention is available at the University of Minnesota Human Rights Library, Available at: http://umn.edu/humanrts/instree/1907d .htm.

17 Muhammad Siddiq Farhang, *Afghanistan dar panj qarn-i akhir* [In Farsi/Dari. A history of Afghanistan in the last five centuries] (Alexandria, VA: Markaz Farhang Sanayi, 1988), p. 776.

18 See "Afghan Modern Diplomacy: The Role of Allama Mahmoud Tarzi and Mohammad Vali Khan Darvazi", Centre for Strategic Studies of the Ministry of Foreign Affairs of Afghanistan (Kabul, 2009).

19 The English translations of these treaties are available in the appendixes of Ludwig W. Adamec, *Afghanistan 1900-1923: A Diplomatic History*, pp. 188–198.

20 Abdul Samad Ghaus, *The Fall of Afghanistan: An Insider's Account* (Oxford: Brassey's, 1988), p. 47.

21 Ibid, 47.

22 Islah newspaper, 8 July 1931, cited in Gregorian, *The Emergence of Modern Afghanistan*, p. 321.

23 Gregorian, *The Emergence of Modern Afghanistan*, p. 321.

24 For text of the treaty, see the *League of Nations Treaty Series*, no. 3611. vol. 157, 370–381.

25 Gregorian, *The Emergence of Modern Afghanistan*, p. 375.

26 In 1941, Iraqi Prime Minister Rashid Ali al-Gaylani invoked the Saadabad Treaty and requested Afghanistan support his country in fighting against British inva- sion. The Afghan Government declined his request on the basis of Afghanistan's declaration of neutrality in 1939. See Muhammad Siddiq Farhang, *Afghanistan dar panj qarn-i akhir*. [In Farsi/Dari. A history of Afghanistan in the last five centuries], p. 646.

27 In August 1939, Nazi Germany and Soviet Russia had signed a non-aggres- sion pact, while the United Kingdom engaged in a "phony war" with Germany. Effectively, Afghanistan's northern and southern neighbours were on different sides of the grand conflict that was then emerging.

28 See Adamec, *Afghanistan's Foreign Affairs to the Mid-Twentieth Century: Relations with the USSR, Germany, and Britain*, pp. 250–251.

29 Ella Maillart, "Afghanistan's Rebirth", *Journal of The Royal Central Asian Society*, 27(2) (April 1940): 224–228, and also see Gregorian, *The Emergence of Modern Afghanistan*, p. 380.

30 As a conservative, pragmatic, and elderly statesman, Prime Minister Hashim was hardly challenged on state policy matters. See Muhammad Siddiq Farhang, *Afghanistan dar panj qarn akhir*, p. 645.

31 The Soviet embassy in Kabul, for example, had invoked the 1931 treaty of neutrality and non-aggression to demand the eviction of nationals of belligerent states.

32 Farhang, *Afghanistan dar panj qarn akhir?*.

33 Peacetime neutrals avoid treaties of alliance with other states that could put them at risk of being a party to a future war or support of war preparations, as such, were the policies of Switzerland, Belgium, and Sweden and to some extend the United States before her entrance into the Second World War. See Wilhelm Wengler, "The Meaning of Neutrality in Peacetime", *McGill Law Journal*, 10(4) (1964): 369–380.

34 After partition of the subcontinent into India and Pakistan, the Afghan Government supported the right of self-determination for Pashtuns and Baluchs residing on the other side of the Durand Line.

35 In 1946, the United States provided its first major financial and technical assistance to Afghanistan in the Helmand Valley irrigation project. Then, in 1948, the US diplomatic mission in Kabul was upgraded to a resident embassy level. Afghanistan joined the UN in 1946. Trade and bilateral cooperation with the Soviet Union, France, Germany, Japan, and Czechoslovakia also expanded. Notwithstanding these developments, Afghanistan remained politically isolated and diplomatically ineffective.

36 After 1955, the suffixes of Mosbat and Fa'al were added to the Persian world of *bitarafi*, reading Bitarafi Mosbat and Bitarafi Fa'al, which means positive neutrality and active neutrality.

37 Amin Saikal, *Modern Afghanistan: A History of Struggle and Survival* (London: I. B. Tauris, 2006), p. 123.

38 Sayed Qassem Reshtia, *Khatirat-e siyasi Sayed Qaseem Reshtia, 1311 to 1371* [The Political Memoirs of Sayed Qaseem Reshtia, 1932–1992] (Virginia: American Speedy Press, 1997), p. 101.

39 A. R. Pazhwak, "Afghanistan's Policy of Non-Alignment", *Kabul Times*, 21 May 1962, p. 2,

40 Sayed Qassem Reshtia, *The Political Memoirs*, p. 101.

41 During his visit to Kabul in 1953, the US Vice President Richard Nixon disapproved Daud's position on Pashtunista. Nixon referred to Afghanistan's neutrality as equivalent to "political leprosy". A year later, US Secretary of State John Foster Dulles refused to offer any military assistance to Foreign Minister Mohammad Naim, Daud's brother, while a huge military assistance programme was approved for Pakistan. See Jeffery J. Roberts, *The Origins of Conflict in Afghanistan* (Westport, CT: Praeger, 2003), p. 147.

42 Reshtia, *The Political Memoirs of Sayed Qaseem Reshtia*, p. 101.

43 Ghaus, *The Fall of Afghanistan: An Insider's Account*, p. 109.

44 US and USSR Relations, Afghanistan section, available on the website of the Association for Diplomatic Studies and Training (ADST), http://adst.org/Readers/Afghanistan.pdf.

45 A top secret instruction was sent by the Soviet Foreign Ministry to its ambassadors in the non-aligned countries to counterbalance Yugoslavia's effort to convene a meeting concerning the invasion of Afghanistan. The excerpt of the cable is available on; http://digitalarchive.wilsoncenter.org/document/112499.

46 V. P Vaidik, "Afghan Non-Alignment: Changing Faces", *International Studies*, 20(1–2) (1981): 239.

47 Olivier Roy, "Has Islamism a Future in Afghanistan?" ed. William Maley, *Fundamentalism Reborn?: Afghanistan and the Taliban* (New York, NY: New York University Press, 1998), p. 210.
48 The three countries that recognised the Taliban government were Pakistan, Saudi Arabia, and the United Arab Emirates. Afghanistan's seat at the United Nations was held by a representative appointed by the Mujahideen government of President Burhannudin Rabbani.
49 In a September 2013 meeting with Kai Eide, former Special Representative of the UN Secretary General for Afghanistan (2008–2010), recalled to the author that, when he used the term "neutrality" in reference to Afghanistan's future international status, President Hamid Karzai rejected the idea as "totally unacceptable". This incident is referred to in his memoir, *Power Struggle Over Afghanistan: An Inside Look at What Went Wrong and What We Can Do to Repair the Damage* (New York: Skyhorse Publishing, Inc., 2013), pp. 138–140. Also, Chinmaya Gharekhan, Karl Inderfurth, and Ashley J. Tellis in a joint paper "Reviewing the Regional Approach to Afghanistan" have pointed to President Karzai's displeasure with the idea of Afghanistan's neutrality as "President Hamid Karzai has expressed reservations about a regional approach based on Afghanistan's future as a permanently neutral state".
50 Nasir A. Andisha, "Neutrality in Afghanistan's Foreign Policy", *USIP*, March 2015.
51 Ibid, p. 12.

5   The analysis of the feasibility and desirability of Afghanistan's permanent neutrality

The previous chapter offered an in-depth reading of the historical dynamics of neutrality/*bitarafi* in Afghanistan's foreign policy in the twentieth century. The study illuminated the deficiencies of the implicit narrative discussed earlier concerning the nature of Afghanistan's traditional neutrality and provided us with the necessary historical insight to address the question of feasibility and desirability of permanent neutrality in the case of Afghanistan.

In order to make the analysis more robust and comprehensive the framework needs to be expanded to include new factors identified throughout the case studies as equally important for the successful maintenance of permanent neutrality.

New factors

One such factor, observed in the case study of Austria, is *the significance of fixed and recognised borders (absence of irredentist claims)*. Austrian permanent neutrality, for example, would not have been technically and practically possible if the Yugoslav claim—backed by the Soviet Union— over the territory of Carinthia had not been solved in advance. Similarly, credibility of Turkmenistan's permanent neutrality has been linked to the absence of irredentist claim *vis-à-vis* its neighbouring states despite the presence of a large number of ethnic Turkmen living across its borders, especially in Iran and Uzbekistan.

Another factor, witnessed in the case study of Laos, is *the absence of active involvement of trans-border non-state actors in the conflict*. The presence of thousands of Vietnamese irregulars and active support networks across the border in North Vietnam made the task of monitoring the implementation of the international agreement on neutrality impossible and thus contributed to the overall failure of the neutrality-based solution in Laos. Moreover, the non-state nature of these support networks provided the

Table 5.1 The revised analytical framework

External factor + Internal factors = Viable permanent neutrality	
External factors/determinants	**Internal factors/determinants**
1. Appropriate geopolitical position and importance	4. Domestic stability and cohesion
2. Appropriate external conditions, balance of power, and military stalemate	5. Capabilities, both military and economic
3. Consensus and agreement of neighbouring countries and the great powers	
Added/New factors	
6. Fixed and agreed-upon borders (absence of irredentist claims)	
7. No active involvement of trans-border non-state actors in the conflict	
8. Cultural and ideological outlook toward permanent neutrality	

North Vietnamese Government with plausible deniability while it repeatedly breached the provisions of the neutrality agreement. And finally, in order to address the cultural-ideological aspects of the feasibility study of a policy of neutrality in a monolithic, conservative society, such as Afghanistan, the analytical framework in the final analysis has to factor in the discussion on the place of neutrality in Siyar (Islamic international law). Hence, before commencing the examination of the research question, the revised analytical framework, also including the three new factors, is set out in Table 5.1.

Furnished with a revised analytical framework, we now return to examination of the main research question.

Feasibility and desirability of Afghanistan's permanent neutrality

In the following section each of the eight determinants/variables of a viable permanent neutrality will be examined on the basis of the appraised historical analysis and the existing strategic and policy discourse on Afghanistan.

External factors/determinants

Before examining the presence of these factors in the case of the current conflict in Afghanistan, let us recall one of the main assumptions of this book: that the conflict in Afghanistan is primarily driven by competing interests of the regional and extra-regional powers. Unlike views grounded in the primacy of cultural, tribal, and ethnic drivers of conflict, the study asserts that the issue of instability in Afghanistan is largely linked to the regional security architecture, Afghanistan's place in it, and external, often proxy, confrontations for dominance fought on Afghanistan's soil. Therefore, an internationally guaranteed declaration of permanent neutrality, which could remove Afghanistan out of the vicious circle of negative external competition, is a way out of the current conflict. However, for such a solution to work, the situation in Afghanistan has to meet the following prerequisites for a viable permanent neutrality.

Geopolitical position and importance

There is a near consensus among the academic and policy circles that Afghanistan's geopolitical position at the intersection of the three regions, South Asia, Central Asia, and the Middle East, has made the country strategically significant for surrounding neighbouring countries and the great powers. It is also well documented that for the most part of its modern history, Afghanistan has played the role of a buffer state between her powerful neighbours. These maxims have sustained two opposite geopolitical views on the future of Afghanistan. Scholars of security and strategic studies classify Afghanistan as an insulator state, which, according to Buzan and Waever, plays its role "by being relatively passive: either marking the zone of indifference or absorbing peripheral energies from the separate Regional Security Complexes (RSCs)".[1] According to this view, given the strategic imperatives and geopolitical configuration of the region, a post-NATO Afghanistan will once again become a contested backyard of the three surrounding security complexes.[2]

However, another group of scholars and policymakers, including the majority of Afghans, challenge the conventional security-centric views of Afghanistan's geopolitics and its role in the region. This group argues that the systemic and socio-economic changes that the region has undergone since the end of the Cold War have transformed Afghanistan's geography from a liability to an asset. Far from being an insulator, the new Afghanistan could very well play the role of an aggregator, connecting the regions it used to separate. Current policies of Afghanistan's government and "the international community" follow this strand of thinking.

Notwithstanding the differences of views on her future prospects, as a rugged, landlocked, and former buffer state, Afghanistan meets the common geographical portrayal of permanently neutral states described throughout this study. In fact, a majority of the proponents of Afghanistan's neutrality, mentioned in Chapter 1, have referred to the country's formidable geography, its past buffer status between the Russian and the British empires and its current geostrategic location at the fault line of the three regions to justify their argument for turning Afghanistan into a permanently neutral state.

In terms of its magnitude and influence, for the purpose of this study, Afghanistan could be classified as a small/weak state. While there is no academic consensus on what constitutes a small state, IR scholars have attempted to create certain quantifiable cut-offs on the basis of size (land and people) and power (economic and military capabilities) to address the issue.[3]

Based on this, and the foregoing historical analysis, it could be argued that Afghanistan generally fits the geographical and power profile of a candidate for permanent neutrality embedded in the first prerequisite of our analytical framework. Also, in terms of its significance to the neighbouring countries and the great powers, Afghanistan has certainly been a strategically significant country but apparently not strategically vital to the interests of the great powers given that it has been abandoned by the great powers at different points throughout history. However, its strategic significance to the core interest of neighbouring states is a topic that needs to be further explored.

Appropriate external conditions, balance of power, and military stalemate

The second condition of viable permanent neutrality is linked solely to external forces at work that directly influence the inception and perpetuation of a conflict. Regardless of whether the motive behind a scheme of neutralisation is either abatement of a conflict or preventing its escalation into a major war, an approximate balance of power among the rival great powers and a military stalemate at the battlefields are the main prerequisites of successful permanent neutrality.

The external drivers of the conflict in Afghanistan could be broadly divided into two levels: an international level of competition and a regional level of competition. At the international level, the main antagonists are the NATO-led Western allies versus the surrounding great powers, such as Russia and China. At the regional level, the major contenders are Pakistan and India. Competition for influence among other regional players, such as Iran, Saudi Arabia, Turkey, the Central Asian Republics, and the Gulf States (though at a less rigorous level), also contributes to the persistence of conflict in Afghanistan. However, for the sake of parsimony, one can group the regional rivals competing inside Afghanistan into two clusters: the Pakistan cluster supported by China and the Gulf Arab states and to some extent Turkey, and the India cluster supported by Russia, Iran, and majority of the Central Asian Republics.

The international sources of conflict in Afghanistan are often discussed in the context of the "New Great Game", a renewed strategic rivalry among the United States, Russia, and China for dominance within the Central Asian region. While all three great players have certain strategic, economic, and political goals in the region, ranging from access to military bases, to concessions with respect to the region's natural resources, to greater political influence, the nature of their relationship inside Afghanistan is more cooperative than competitive. The three great powers are neither actively belligerent nor directly involved in supporting the opposing forces in the conflict in Afghanistan. To the contrary, as permanent members of the United Nations Security Council, they endorse and support the ongoing international missions in Afghanistan.

As the nature of international competition in Afghanistan, and its impact on the current conflict, is apparently not at a level to necessitate the declaration of neutrality by Afghanistan to defuse their negative influence, it is not required to examine the presence of the *balance of power* and *military stalemate* at an international level. The main causes of the conflict are arguably linked to the dynamic of the rivalry among the regional powers.

At the regional level, it is argued that the two clusters of players—a Pakistan-led cluster and an India-led cluster—are involved, often in an almost zero-sum competition for increased political and economic influence inside Afghanistan. An alternative view of the conflict, predominant among Afghans, places the blame squarely on Pakistan's interference in Afghanistan's affairs and its misguided policy of acquiring a "strategic depth" in the country. We return to this view in the next section; however, at this stage we examine the presence of the determinants of neutrality—the *balance of power* and *military stalemate*—in the context of the ongoing regional competition.

Based on the current literature, despite a wide gap in traditional means of power, such as size, population, and resources in favour of India, a balance of power (balance of terror) has emerged between India and Pakistan following the nuclear tests conducted by both countries in May 1998. Similarly, in terms of combined (soft and hard) measures of influence in the domestic political and security dynamics inside Afghanistan, one can safely argue that both camps stand on roughly equal footing.[4] Thus, at the regional level, the situation meets the prerequisite of an approximate balance of power set forth in our revised analytical framework. While this strategic balance of power between the rival groups may result in preventing any side from fully dominating the situation, it is hard to argue whether it will lead to stabilisation of the conflict or its perpetuation.

For the time being, contrary to claims about a general fatigue among the Taliban forces, stalemate on the ground, and realisation by their political leaders that victory through military means is impossible, there is no sign of a sense of military stalemate in the battlefields. In fact, past three years have seen the bloodiest and most violent campaign in the past decade. The Taliban and the military establishment in Pakistan appear to believe that, with the departure of the US/NATO forces from Afghanistan and by intensification of their military offensives, victory of some sort is on the horizon. Hence, the existing conditions on the ground fail to meet the prerequisite of a military stalemate.

If the current balance of power in the region, further reinforced by external balancers such as the United States and China, produces a military stalemate on the battlefields and a realisation among regional players that domination is not possible no matter how long and how hard one side tries, it could create a situation conducive to neutrality-based solutions. Otherwise, a balance of power among the regional players with no sign of a military stalemate on the ground may result in the continuation of conflict in Afghanistan and its spread into contiguous areas.

Consensus and agreement of neighbouring countries and the great powers

The third precondition of a viable permanent neutrality identified in the analytical framework hinges on the emergence of a consensus among major external stakeholders that the neutralisation of the contested state serves their interest better than the status quo.

Some Western and regional policy and academic circles agree that turning Afghanistan into a permanently neutral state has the potential to reduce the regional rivalries and lead to termination of the conflict in the country. Former US Secretaries of State, Henry Kissinger and Hillary Clinton, former high-profile American diplomats such as James Dobbins, Karl Inderfurth, Peter Tomsen, and Dennis Kux, former Indian diplomats such as Hamid Ansari (also former Vice President) and Chinmaya Gharekhan, former Pakistani Ambassador Aziz Ahmad Khan and Kai Eide, former Special Representative of the Secretary General of the United Nations for Afghanistan, among others, have argued in favour of a neutrality-based solution for the crisis in Afghanistan. However, these views do not represent the official positions of their respective governments *vis-à-vis* the need for neutralisation of Afghanistan.

Among all major external stakeholders, the Russian Federation is perhaps the only country that has declared that neutrality for Afghanistan is its official policy position.[5] Iran, in principle, would prefer to see Afghanistan become a neutral country rather than turn into a platform for foreign intervention in the region. However, according to a senior Iranian diplomat and expert on Afghanistan, Iran has no illusions about Afghanistan's ability to maintain its neutrality given the level of its economic and military dependence on foreign sources. Afghanistan needs to prepare for neutrality by building a domestic consensus and reducing its severe aid dependency, the diplomat lamented.[6]

Of all the regional stakeholders with whom this author spoke while researching a report on "Neutrality in Afghanistan's Foreign Policy",[7] the Pakistanis seemed more ambivalent and cynical toward the prospect of a neutral Afghanistan. While thinly praising Afghanistan's neutral position during its wars with India in 1965 and 1971, in a regional context, the Pakistani elite—politicians, former military, media, and civil society representatives—do not consider a neutral Afghanistan as either a desirable outcome or a feasible solution to the current crisis in the country. They emphasised that even if, in principle, the Pakistani state commits to respecting Afghanistan's neutrality, in practice it is incapable of controlling the movement of hostile non-state actors across the porous frontiers between the two countries. Therefore, a more desirable approach, according to these interlocutors, would be to improve bilateral relationships by building institutional linkages and fostering commercial partnerships.

However, when it comes to the future of international engagement in Afghanistan, Pakistani leaders have frequently insisted that "[t]he historic neutrality of Afghanistan should be maintained with the commitment that Afghan soil will not be used against any of its neighbours".[8] This double standard approach of Pakistan toward Afghanistan's neutrality, its continuous support for terrorist groups inside the country despite enormous international pressure and at the cost of domestic stability, apparently indicates that assuring its primacy in Afghanistan remains of vital interest to Pakistan.

Similarly, policymakers in India have no better attitude toward the enterprise of neutralisation of Afghanistan. The predominant view in New Delhi is that since Afghanistan has historically remained neutral in the regional conflicts and has committed to not allow its territory to be used against any of its neighbours, a formal declaration of permanent neutrality is both irrelevant and impractical. Since India has made enormous investment and enjoys greater respect and trust in Afghanistan, the idea of neutrality, which subtly implies that India is a party to the proxy conflict, irritates Indian policy circles.

Discussions with the Afghanistan expert community in India, including those who previously supported neutrality, revealed that their neutrality proposal met with official disapproval. A former Ambassador and advocate of a neutrality-based solution to the crisis in Afghanistan reported in conversation with this author that the Indian Government and President Karzai did not like the idea of neutrality, "so we were told not to pursue it further". Another former Ambassador argued that while what neutrality implied for fostering regional cooperation was more important than the meaning that was attached to the term, "you [Afghanistan] have to drop the term neutrality", which appears to have aroused suspicion, in favour of something more economically and politically attractive.

China maintained a limited bilateral engagement and for the most part has adhered to its official foreign policy mantra of non-aggression and non-interference in the country's internal affairs in its dealings with Afghanistan. In the past, Chinese officials raised their concern *vis-à-vis* the purpose and duration of the US bases in Afghanistan or what they called "militarisation of the region" and have occasionally demanded that Afghanistan should be kept neutral and outside the sphere of influence of any power. However, most recently China has taken a more active role in fostering regional cooperation and supporting Afghanistan's peace and reconciliation efforts.

Despite some level of support for neutrality among the policymakers and academia in the West and in the region, overall, the idea of turning Afghanistan into a neutral state is not underpinned by the grand elite consensus required for neutrality. Securing an agreement among such a diverse group, particularly when some of the main stakeholders are engaged in a fierce rivalry with each other inside and outside Afghanistan, is inconceivable in the short term. Moreover, given increased hostility between the West and Russia in Ukraine, the disagreement over conflict in Syria and the rise of ISIL, there is neither an appetite nor sufficient political capital at the disposal of any of the major stakeholders to produce an agreement on neutralisation of Afghanistan and to guarantee its implementation. The analysis thus far indicates that except for its geographical profile and presence of an approximate regional balance of power, the situation fails to meet the other external determinants of viable permanent neutrality.

Internal factors/determinants

Stability and cohesion

Except for a period of relative stability between 2002 and 2005, Afghanistan has suffered from persistent and large-scale violence since the Soviet invasion in 1979. Over the past five years, according to a 2019 report by the United Nations Assistance Mission (UNAMA) and the International Crisis Group, the level of violence and casualties has been on the rise. Civilian casualties increased by 11 per cent compared to the previous year. Similarly, a report by BBC in January 2019 quoting President Ghani puts casualties of the Afghanistan Security Forces since 2014 at 45,000, the highest figure in recent years. The Taliban, and other terrorist groups, have mounted high-profile attacks on provincial capitals, district headquarters and security checkpoints throughout the country. While in the past high-level violence was mostly confined to provinces in the south and the east of the country, recently the conflict has spread into the north and north-eastern provinces. In the majority of the highly volatile provinces bordering Pakistan, the government's writ does not extend much beyond the district centres. The level of casualties, attacks, and limited government control indicates that currently Afghanistan lacks the minimum level of stability needed to pursue a policy of neutrality.

Since permanent neutrality severs a country's sovereignty and limits its foreign policy options, devising and adopting such a policy requires a strong national consensus among various domestic stakeholders. Based on the discussions with former and current Afghan policymakers, and on the examination of the secondary sources, it is evident that the general attitude toward neutrality and its utility as a tool for ending the conflict in Afghanistan is not encouraging.

While in the past, Afghanistan's principle of *bitarafi*/neutrality enjoyed overwhelming elite and popular support, and often formed the basis of domestic consensus on foreign policy matters, in the current environment, where the majority of Afghans recognise that their country's military and economic vulnerability favours some form of ties with the West, permanent neutrality has few if any serious sympathisers. For example, the Karzai administration deliberately avoided any discussion of neutrality in reference to Afghanistan's future status. Former President Hamid Karzai was particularly contemptuous of the idea of Afghanistan's neutrality and called its inclusion in the official discourse on the future of Afghanistan as "totally unacceptable".[9] Similarly, the top security and foreign policy officials in the previous government questioned the logic of "traditional neutrality" and rejected the assertions that neutrality was always the most suitable foreign policy option for Afghanistan. On the contrary, some of these senior officials argued that had Afghanistan joined the Western-led alliances and had Afghanistan maintained a more strategic attitude toward its relationship with the United States, the country would not have been too exposed to a Soviet invasion.[10]

However, as alluded to in Chapter 1, in November 2013, a group of high-profile Afghan politicians, former diplomats, and civil society leaders, including some senior members of what is now the National Unity Government (NUG), endorsed a vision of "Afghan-led and Afghanistan-specific enduring neutrality" at a Track 2 regional peace and stability forum.[11] This move raised some expectations that the NUG might be more amenable to neutrality-based solutions. Yet, when asked about Afghanistan's neutrality being compromised by signing of the Bilateral Security Agreements (BSA) with the United States and NATO, President Ashraf Ghani in a side event to the Munich Security Forum in December 2014 called neutrality "a term from the 1950s"[12] and questioned its applicability in the contemporary international setting. In April 2015, in an unprecedented move, President Ghani announced Afghanistan's support for the Saudi-led coalition in its war against Houthis-led forces in Yemen, removing any illusion of adhering to Afghanistan's "traditional neutrality" in regional affairs.

Hence, despite neutrality historically being considered a principle of Afghanistan's foreign policy, in contemporary Afghanistan the concept of neutrality has failed to take root either as an ideal for social cohesion or as a means for solving the existing conflict.

Military and economic capabilities

Afghanistan National Defence and Security Forces (ANDSF), consisting of the army, the police, and the Intelligence Special Forces, stand at nearly 352,000 strong. This force is aided by another 30,000 local police personnel. In terms of its size and fighting spirit, the ANDSF is a formidable force to reckon with. However, in terms of its capabilities, it is a light infantry force for fighting insurgency and providing basic security, not an army capable of conducting full-spectrum operations in conventional wars. In critical areas, such as air support, intelligence, surveillance and reconnaissance, logistics, ammunition, spare parts, and even fuel for vehicles and power generators, the Afghan armed forces are still highly dependent on US/NATO assistance. On the funding side, out of the current US$5.1 billion of annual military expenditure, the Afghan Government contributes less than 10 per cent to its annual military expenditure; the rest is paid by the United States and its NATO allies and partner countries.

With a per capita GDP of US$664.8 and one-third of its population living below the poverty line, Afghanistan is the second poorest country in Asia. For more than a decade, the Afghan economy has been heavily reliant on foreign aid. Some 90 per cent of the country's GDP is linked to foreign aid and foreign military expenditure. In the past four years, nearly 60 per cent of Afghanistan's core budget and almost all of its development expenditure has been funded by donor countries. A staggering 56 per cent of the workforce is either unemployed or under-employed, and the size of the labour force is increasing due to a rapid population growth.[13]

Lack of proper infrastructure, poor security, and regulatory and political bottlenecks inside Afghanistan, as well as in neighbouring countries, is hampering the prospects for economic growth and realisation of the country's potential as a regional hub for trade and transit in goods and energy. Hence, given the current level of poverty and reliance on foreign military and economic assistance, Afghanistan does not meet the minimum threshold for viable permanent neutrality set by our analytical framework.

The foregoing analysis of external and internal determinants of viable permanent neutrality already reveals how untenable the prospect of making Afghanistan a neutral state appears to be.

New factors/determinates

Fixed and agreed-upon borders

As the experience of the three prominent permanent neutral and other neutral states reviewed earlier indicates, absence of irredentist ambitions on the part of the candidate state and its neighbouring states, and the existence of fixed and agreed-upon international borders are vital prerequisites for declaration of permanent neutrality. Neutrality agreements have always had a strong emphasis on mutual recognition and respect for territorial integrity of candidates and the guarantors' states. Similarly, proposals for neutralisation of Afghanistan, reviewed in Chapter 1, and the recent suggestion for a neutrality-based solution for the crisis in Ukraine, have underlined the issue of recognition and respect for current international borders.[14]

Given Afghanistan's long-running disputes, first with British India and later with Pakistan, over its eastern and southern frontier, commonly known as the Durand Line, meeting this prerequisite is perhaps the most challenging hurdle facing the prospect of Afghanistan's neutrality. The approximately 2,640 km long line, enacted under the 1893 Durand-Abdul Rahman Agreement, politically divided the Pashtun and Baluch tribes into Afghanistan and British India's spheres of influence. While the line was supposedly intended to specify the limits of each side's spheres of influence in the tribal areas, British India affirmed its dominion and consolidated its grip over the region through subsequent British-Afghanistan treaties of 1905, 1919, and 1921.[15]

The dispute over the legal status of the Durand Line took a new twist when in 1947 the newly created state of Pakistan declared the line as its international border with Afghanistan. The Afghan government refused to recognise the line as an international border and initially abstained from recognising Pakistan's statehood. Drawing on the vague legal status of the Durand Line as an international border and emphasising the principle of self-determination for post-colonial regions, Afghanistan insisted that, during the 1947 referendum, the Pashtun inhabitants of British India, beside the options of joining either India or Pakistan, should have been given a choice of forming an independent state. As tensions between Afghanistan and Pakistan heightened, in July 1949 an Afghan Grand Assembly (*Loya Jirga*) repudiated the Durand Agreement and the subsequent treaties and called for creation of an independent state of Pashtunistan. While major world powers, such as the United States and the United Kingdom supported Pakistan's position, successive Afghan governments have since refused to recognise the Durand Line officially as an international border.

Most scholars and policymakers believe that the dispute over the status of the Durand Line remains a constant source of hostility between

Afghanistan and Pakistan and has contributed to instability and prolonged conflict in the region.

Without tangible incentives, recognition of the Durand Line, as well as committing to a policy of permanent neutrality, is considered a lose-lose scenario for Afghanistan to which no Afghan Government could possibly commit itself. Hence, finding an amicable solution to the issue of the Durand Line is a prerequisite for achieving meaningful neutrality.

Based on the preceding elucidations and given the highly securitised and thorny issue of the Durand Line, Afghanistan fails to meet yet another prerequisite for successful permanent neutrality concerning fixed borders and lack of territorial disputes.

No active involvement of violent trans-border non-state actors in the conflict

One of the major factors that contributed to the failure of Laotian neutralisation efforts was the presence of trans-border militias. Similarly, in Afghanistan, active involvement of violent trans-border non-state actors in the conflict and existence of support structures across the borders are the prominent features of the nearly four-decade-long war in Afghanistan. After the Soviet invasion in 1979, the Afghan war (Jihad) attracted hundreds of foreign fighters, mostly from the Arab world, to fight alongside the Afghan Mujahideen against the Soviet forces. The fighters, known as the "Afghan Arabs",[16] formed several terrorist networks across the region, of which Al Qaeda became the most prominent one. To facilitate the war inside Afghanistan, the Pakistani Government, with funds from the Western and Arab states, built extensive support structures, including training and recruitment centres in the tribal areas of Pakistan.

These support structures, particularly hundreds of Madrasas (religious seminar) and training centres, were later used by Pakistan to raise the Taliban movement in the mid-1990s and facilitate their campaign of terror inside Afghanistan. The sanctuaries across the border still function as safe havens for dozens of violent trans-border non-state groups, such as the Taliban (both Afghan and Pakistani branches), the Haqqani network, Al Qaeda, the Islamic Movement of Uzbekistan (IMU), the East Turkestan Independence Movement (ETIM), the ISIL-affiliated Khorasan group, and other smaller splinter outfits.

During discussions with regional experts on the possibility of Afghanistan's neutrality, the presence of these groups, and their traditional support networks in the tribal areas, were among the top concerns raised by sceptics about Afghanistan's neutrality. Pakistani interlocutors emphasised that even if the Pakistani state recognised Afghanistan's neutrality and committed to respecting it, there would be no guarantee that the violent trans-border non-state actors residing within the country would remain neutral in Afghan affairs. Indian experts had serious doubts about Pakistan's willingness and ability to dismantle the Taliban and Al Qaeda sanctuaries from inside its territory and prevent their cross-border movement. Generally, there was a near consensus among all discussants that Afghanistan's declaration of permanent neutrality, and Pakistan's official recognition of it, would be meaningless until both states were capable of reining in these groups and controlling their territory, particularly the border regions.

Since neutrality as an instrument of conflict resolution was seen as fit for particular types of states and circumstances where states are perceived to be the sole actors, and agreement among stakeholder states is sufficient to guarantee neutrality, an eminent presence of non-state actors and insurgent groups in the Afghan conflict, and existence of entrenched support structures across the border in Pakistan, render the policy of neutrality unworkable.

Cultural and ideological outlook toward permanent neutrality

The final prerequisite identified in the revised analytical framework is connected to the compatibility of the concept of permanent neutrality with the prevailing cultural and ideological outlook of the population in the candidate state. While this factor may not be very influential in democratic, multicultural, and multi-faith societies, it is of peculiar significance for Muslim-majority states where it is established that major policies should not contradict Islamic law.

Afghanistan, though not officially following Sharia law, is one such state where Islam is entrenched in the culture, traditions, and legal system.[17] Major policies, if they explicitly contravened the tenets of Islamic jurisprudence, would have no chance of ratification or implementation. For example, the ill-fated policies of the communist regime, such as land reform and compulsory female education, contributed, among other things, to the religious scholars' call for a Jihad against the regime in the 1980s.

The modern scholars of Islamic international law (Siyar) see no objection in the adoption of a policy of neutrality by an Islamic polity on a temporary basis. However, there are ample textual sources, if not practical examples, to prove that declaration of permanent neutrality is against the fundamental principles of an Islamic society, particularly in case of a blatant aggression against a weak Muslim state, and when one country's neutrality could endanger the unity of the Muslim Ummah.

Given the dominance of conservative and religious forces in the social, political, and cultural layers of Afghan society and state, and considering the lessons learnt from controversial policies of the previous regimes, declaration of permanent neutrality and its preservation would be highly improbable, if not outright impossible.

Conclusion

Given Afghanistan's geopolitical position at the fault line of great power conflict and considering the positive experience of permanent neutrality of states such as Switzerland and Austria in avoiding great power conflict on their soil, neutrality might appear to be a desirable undertaking for Afghanistan. However, the findings of this research reveal that the country fails to meet the majority of both the material and the ideational criteria embodied in the analytical framework as foundations for a viable permanent neutrality.

One can argue that while the discussion of Afghanistan's neutrality as a post-withdrawal policy gained some momentum during 2009 and 2010, due to the challenges surveyed in this study the idea was subsequently abandoned. Instead, the concept of a grand regional gathering, espoused by the proponents of neutrality, was transformed by the end of 2011 into a regional confidence-building and cooperation forum known as the Istanbul Process. On the security side, by signing a Security and Defence Cooperation Agreement with the United States and a Status of Forces Agreement (SoFA) with NATO in September 2014, the Afghan Government granted military bases and freedom of action for counter-terrorism operations to US and NATO forces inside Afghanistan. This, legally and conceptually, left little, if any room, for discussion of permanent neutrality for Afghanistan until a complete withdrawal of the foreign forces is realised.

Nonetheless, there is a general understanding among a majority of Afghan and foreign policymakers that though a continuation of international support is vital to sustainability of Afghan state institutions, to achieve lasting peace and stability and to realise the benefits of regional cooperation in and around Afghanistan, it is equally important to keep exploring internationally backed regional neutrality and non-aggression arrangements. This, rather than the permanent neutrality of a single state, is the more realistic policy path to pursue. And ultimately, considering Afghanistan's geography as a constant factor and given the primacy of geopolitical motives in the strategic calculation of the great powers, to achieve a broad regional cooperation arrangement, Afghanistan has to find a way to institutionalise a regional balance of interests. As the prospect for a political settlement of the conflict in Afghanistan is rising, an internationally backed regional *treaty of guaranteeing peace and non-aggression* could serve as a diplomatic instrument for assuring inclusive regional cooperation and peace in and around Afghanistan.

Closing thoughts

As observed, *neutrality* is a complicated term. When used in policy discussion, it proves to have complex dimensions beyond the basic idea of *lack of commitment* that its ordinary-language use has made relatively familiar. This analysis of feasibility and desirability of permanent neutrality as a diplomatic solution and foreign policy choice for vulnerable states could be expanded even further. Senior Western diplomats and strategists continue to propose a form of neutrality as a possible solution to conflicts in states located on the geopolitical fault lines, such as Ukraine, Georgia, Afghanistan, and others. They argue that these areas, while strategically significant for the United States and its NATO allies, are not strategically vital to their interest. A compromised solution in the form of *permanent neutrality* in which the core interests of regional powers are taken into consideration would be necessary for maintenance of regional stability and global order.

This concise academic and historical background to the concept and practice of neutrality could hopefully jump start debates on the feasibility of the idea of "new neutrality". I close the study with a challenge: if neutrality has functioned as a relatively successful conflict resolution tool during the Cold War, can a reframed and adopted version of neutrality serve the needs of the twenty-first-century world order and potentially prevent the re-emergence of what is often termed as the "new cold war"?

Notes

1 Barry Buzan and Ole Wæver, *Regions and Powers: The Structure of International Security* (Cambridge: Cambridge University Press, 2003), p. 485.
2 See Barry Buzan, "The South Asian Security Complex in a Decentring World Order: Reconsidering Regions and Powers Ten Years On", *International Studies*, 4(1) (January 2011): 1–19. Kristian Berg Harpviken, "Caught in the Middle? Regional Perspectives on Afghanistan", ed. Kristian Berg Harpviken, *Troubled Regions and Failing States: The Clustering and Contagion of Armed Conflicts* (Comparative Social Research, Volume 27, Bingley-UK: Emerald Group Publishing Limited, 2010), 277–305 and Shahrbanou Tadjbakhsh, "The Persian Gulf and Afghanistan: Iran and Saudi Arabia's Rivalry Projected", *PRIO Paper* (Oslo: PRIO, 2013).
3 For more information on definition and classification of "small states", see Tom Crowards, "Defining the Category of 'Small' States", *Journal of International Development*, 14 (2002): 143–179 and Matthias Maass, "The Elusive Definition of the Small State", *International Politics*, 46 (2009): 65–83.
4 While India and Iran enjoy more soft/political influence, Pakistan and Saudi Arabia appear to hold more hard/ideological-militancy influence in Afghanistan.
5 In his statement delivered at the Kabul International Conference on 20 July 2010, the Russian Foreign Minister Sergey Lavrov reiterated his country's position on the subject of Afghanistan's neutrality by saying, "The restoration of the neutral

status of Afghanistan is designed to become one of the key factors of creating an atmosphere of good-neighbourly relations and cooperation in the region … We expect that this idea will be supported by the Afghan people. The presidents of Russia and the US have already come out in favor of it". See "Afghanistan dreams of a NATO-free future", *Russia Today*,23 July 2010. Available at: http://rt.com/usa/afghanistan-nato-free-future.

6 Author's conversation with a senior Iranian diplomat in Kabul, March 2014.

7 Andisha, "Neutrality in Afghanistan's Foreign Policy", *A USIP Special Report*, March 2015. http://usip.org/sites/default/files/SR360-Neutrality-in-Afghanistan's-Foreign-Policy.pdf.

8 "Gilani for 'neutrality' of Afghanistan in future initiative", *Indian Express*, 10 January 2010. http://archive.indianexpress.com/news/gilani-for-neutrality-of-afghanistan-in-future-initiative/565605/.

9 Kai Eide, *Power Struggle Over Afghanistan: An Inside Look at What Went Wrong and What We Can Do to Repair the Damage* (New York: Skyhorse Publishing, Inc., 2013), pp. 138–140.

10 Author's private conversation with current and former senior Afghan ministers in Canberra and Kabul. April–August 2013.

11 "Afghanistan's Region: 2014 & Beyond, Joint Declaration on regional Peace and Stability", 17 November 2013. Available at: library.fes.de/pdf-files/iez/10307.pdf.

12 Transcript of President Ghani's Lecture at Chatham House (The Royal Institute of International Affairs) "Fixing Failed States: From Theory to Practice", 4 December 2014.

13 Anthony Cordesman, "The Afghan War in 2013: Meeting the Challenges of Transition. Volume II, Afghan Economics and Outside Aid", Center for Strategic and International Studies, March 2013.

14 Graham Allison, "A 'Belgian Solution' for Ukraine?" *The National Interest*, 15 March 2014. Available at: http://nationalinterest.org/commentary/%E2%80%9Cbelgian-solution%E2%80%9D-ukraine-10062.

15 The 1905 (Anglo-Afghan pact), signed by Amir Habibullah in April 1905 with the mission led by Sir Louis Dane, 1919 (Treaty of Rawalpindi), signed on 8 August 1919, by the Afghan peace mission sent to Rawalpindi to conclude the third Afghan War, and 1921 (Anglo-Afghan Treaty), concluded by the Dobbs Mission in Kabul, 22 November 1921.

16 Stephen E. Atkins, *Encyclopedia of Modern Worldwide Extremists and Extremist Groups* (Westport, Conn: Greenwood Publishing Group, 2004), p. 11.

17 Article 3 of Afghanistan's Constitution emphasises that "[n]o law shall contravene the tenets and provisions of the holy religion of Islam in Afghanistan". The Constitution of the Islamic Republic of Afghanistan, Ratified on 26 January 2004.

Bibliography

Abdullaev, Kamoluding and Akbarzadeh, Shahram. *Historical Dictionary of Tajikistan*. 2nd ed., Lanham, MD: Scarecrow Press, April 2010.

Adamec, Ludwig W. *Historical Dictionary of Afghanistan*. London: Scarecrow Press, 1991.

"Afghan Modern Diplomacy: The Role of Allama Mahmoud Tarzi and Mohammad Vali Khan Darvazi". Kabul: Centre for Strategic Studies of the Ministry of Foreign Affairs of Afghanistan, 2009.

"Agenda Item 3J the Austrian State Treaty". In: *Foreign Ministers Meeting; Berlin Discussions*, January 25 to February 18, 1954, Washington, DC: Superintendent of Documents, 1954, U.S. Government Printing Office, 233–234.

Agius, Christine. *The Social Construction of Swedish Neutrality: Challenges to Swedish Identity and Sovereignty*. Manchester: Manchester University Press, 2006.

Agius, Christine and Devine, Karen. "Neutrality: A Really Dead Concept? A Reprise". *Cooperation and Conflict* 46(3) (2011): 265–284.

Akhir, H.D.H.J. "The law of neutrality. A comparative study of Islamic law and public international law". (PhD, University of Malaya, 1984).

Alker, Hayward R., Gurr, Ted Robert, and Rupesinghe, Kumar. *Journeys through Conflict: Narratives and Lessons*. Lanham, MD: Rowman & Littlefield, 2001.

Allard, Sven. *Russia and the Austrian State Treaty: A Case Study of Soviet Policy in Europe*. University Park, PA: Pennsylvania State University Press, 1970.

Allison, Graham. "A 'Belgian Solution' for Ukraine?" *The National Interest*, 15 March 2014.

Al-Rodhan, Nayef R.F. and Kuepfer, Sara. *Stability of States: Nexus Between Transnational Threats, Globalization, and Internal Resilience*. Genève: Slatkine Edition, 2007.

Altfeld, Michael F. and de Mesquita, Bruce Bueno. "Choosing Sides in Wars". *International Studies Quarterly* 23(1) (1979): 87–112.

Andisha, Nasir A. "Neutrality in Afghanistan's Foreign Policy". *Special Report*. The United States Institute of Peace, 2015.

Atkins, Stephen E. *Encyclopedia of Modern Worldwide Extremists and Extremist Groups*. Westport, Conn: Greenwood Publishing Group, 2004.

Barfield, Thomas. *Afghanistan: A Cultural and Political History*. Princeton, NJ: Princeton University Press, 2010.

Bauslaugh, Robert A. *The Concept of Neutrality in Classical Greece*. Berkeley, CA: University of California Press, 1991.

Black, Cyril E., Falk, Richard A., Knorr, Klaus, and Young, Oran. *Neutralization and World Politics*. Princeton, NJ: Princeton University Press, 1968.

Bonjour, Edgar. *Swiss Neutrality: Its History and Meaning*, Translated by M. Hottinger. London: Allen & Unwin, 1946.

Bouvier, John. *A Law Dictionary*, Adapted to the constitution and laws of the United States of America, and of the several states of the American union: With references to the civil and other systems of foreign law, Philadelphia, PA: T. & J.W. Johnson, Law Booksellers, 1843. Two volumes. First volume's reprinted by The Lawbook Exchange, Ltd. Clark New Jersey, 2004.

Bouzenita, Anke I. "The Principle of Neutrality and 'Islamic International Law' (Siyar)". *Global Jurist* 11(1) (2011): 1–34.

Brackett, David S. "International Relations à La Carte: A New Swiss Neutrality in Europe". *Weather Head Centre for International Affairs, Harvard University, WCFIA Working Paper 4*, 1997.

Buchholz, Benjamin. "Thoughts on Afghanistan's Loya Jirga: A Myth?" *Asien* 104 (July 2007): 23–33.

Burne, Owen Tudor. "British Agents in Afghanistan, 1879". Digitized Afghanistan Materials in English from the Arthur Paul Afghanistan Collection. Paper 12, 18 October 2012.

Butler, C.T. and Rothstein, A. *On Conflict and Consensus: A Hand Book of Formal Consensus Decision Making*. 3rd ed. Mountain View, CA: Creative Commons, 2007.

Buzan, Barry and Wæver, Ole. *Regions and Powers: The Structure of International Security*. Cambridge: Cambridge University Press, 2003.

Carafano, James Jay. *Waltzing Into the Cold War: The Struggle for Occupied Austria*. College Station, TX: Texas A&M University Press, 2002.

Chay, John and Ross, Thomas E. eds. *Buffer States in World Politics*. Boulder, CO: Westview Press, 1986.

Chevallaz, Georges-Andre. *The Challenge of Neutrality: Diplomacy and the Defence of Switzerland*. Lanham, MD: Lexington Books, 2001.

Colley, Wellesley Richard and Martin, Robert Montgomery, eds. *The Despatches, Minutes, and Correspondence of the Marquess Wellesley, K.G., During His Administration in India – 5 Volume Set*, 1837.

"Convention Signed on August 31, 1907, between Great Britain and Russia, Containing Arrangements on the Subject of Persia, Afghanistan and Tibet". *The American Journal of International Law* 1(4) (October 1907): 398–406.

Cordesman, Anthony. "The Afghan War in 2013: Meeting the Challenges of Transition. Volume II, Afghan Economics and Outside Aid". Center for Strategic and International Studies, March 2013.

Cronin, Audrey Kurth. "East-West Negotiations over Austria in 1949: Turning-Point in the Cold War". *Journal of Contemporary History* 24(1) (January 1989): 125–145.

Cronin, Audery Kurth. "Thinking Long on Afghanistan: Could It Be Neutralized?" *The Washington Quarterly* 36(1) (2013): 55–72.

Crowards, Tom. "Defining the Category of 'Small' States". *Journal of International Development* 14(2) (2002): 143–179.

Dallin, David J. *Soviet Foreign Policy after Stalin*. Philadelphia, PA: Lippincott, 1961.

Davidson, Apollon. "Russia and South Africa Before the Soviet Era". *Working Papers*. National Research University, Higher School of Economics, 2013.

Dehn, C. G. "The Problem of Neutrality." *Transactions of the Grotius Society* 31 (1945): pp. 139–149. JSTOR, www.jstor.org/stable/743275. Accessed 18 June 2020.

Devine, Karen. "A Comparative Critique of the Practice of Irish Neutrality in the 'Unneutral' Discourse". *Irish Studies in International Affairs* 19(1) (2008): 73–97.

Devine, Karen. "Stretching the IR Theoretical Spectrum on Irish Neutrality: A Critical Social Constructivist Framework". *International Political Science Review* 29(4) (September 2008): 461–488.

Dombey, Daniel and Green, Matthew. "US Aims to Turn Afghanistan into Neutral Zone". *The Financial Times*, 27 June 2011.

Dommen, Arthur J. *Conflict in Laos: The Politics of Neutralisation*. London: Pall Mall Press, 1964.

Dreyer, John and Jesse, Neal G. "Swiss Neutrality Examined: Model, Exception or Both?" *The Journal of Military and Strategic Studies* 15(3) (June 2014): 60–83.

Dupree, Louis. "Myth and Reality in Afghan Neutralism". *Central Asian Survey* 7(2–3) (1988): 2–3.

Eide, Kai. *Power Struggle Over Afghanistan: An Inside Look at What Went Wrong and What We Can Do to Repair the Damage*. New York: Skyhorse Publishing, Inc., 2013.

Evans, David. *Sherman's Horsemen: Union Cavalry Operations in the Atlanta Campaign*. Bloomington, IN: Indiana University Press, 1999.

Fadal, Khaled Abou El. *The Great Theft: Wrestling Islam from the Extremists*. New York, NY: Harper Collins Publishers, 2005.

Fall, Bernard F. "Reappraisal in Laos". *Current History* 42 (January 1962): 8–14.

Faloon, Brian S. "Aspects of Finnish Neutrality". *Irish Studies in International Affairs* 1(3) (1982): 3–12.

Farhang, Siddiq Mohammad. *Afghanistan Dar panj qarn-i Akhi"r*. [In Farsi/Dari. *A History of Afghanistan in the Last Five Centuries*]. Alexandria, VA: Markaz Farhang Sanayi, 1988.

Fischer, Thomas. "Switzerland: Invention of Permanent Neutrality". In: Igor S. Novaković, ed. *Neutrality in the 21st Century – Lesson for Serbia*. Belgrade: ISAC Fond, 2013.

Freedman, Robert O. *Moscow and the Middle East: Soviet Policy since the Invasion of Afghanistan*. Cambridge: Cambridge University Press, 1991.

Gabriel, Jürg Martin. "Neutrality and Neutralism in Southeast Asia, 1960–1970". *Eidgenössische Technische Hochschule, Forschungsstelle für Internationale Beziehungen* 9 (2002): 1–33.

Gémes, Andreas. "Deconstruction of a Myth? Austria and the Hungarian Refugees of 1956–57". In: S. Dempsey and D. Nichols, eds. *Time: Memory, and Cultural Change*. Vienna: IWM Junior Visiting Fellows' Conferences, 2009.

Geoffrey, Butler and Maccoby, S. *The Development of International Law*, London: Longmans, 1928.

Ghaus, Samad Abdul. *The Fall of Afghanistan: An Insider's Account*. Oxford: Brassey, 1988.

Goetschel, Laurant. "Neutrality, a Really Dead Concept?" *Cooperation and Conflict* 34(2) (1999): 115–139.

Graham, James. "Military Power vs Economic Power in History". *HistoryOrb.com*, January 2014.

Gregorian, Vartan. *The Emergence of Modern Afghanistan*. Stanford, Calif: Stanford University Press, 1969. Verse 29 and 74 of Chapter 9, (Surat al taubah), *The Holy Qur'an*. The University of Leeds: Qurany Tool.

Haas, Jasef. "60 Years of Marshall Plan Aid – A Critical Appraisal from an Austrian Perspective". *Monetary Policy & the Economy* 2 (2007): 126–139.

Hague Convention (V) Respecting the Rights and Duties of Neutral Powers and Persons in Case of War on Land, U.S.T.S. 540, 2 A.J.I.L. Supp. 117, entered into force January 26, 1910.

Halbrook, Stephen. *Target Switzerland: Swiss Armed Neutrality in World War II*. New York, NY: Sarpedeon, 1998.

Halbrook, Stephen P. *Target Switzerland: Swiss Armed Neutrality in World War II*. Cambridge, Mass: Da Capo Press, 2004.

Hamidullah, Muhammad. *Muslim Conduct of State*. Kazi Publications, 1992.

Hanggi, Hiener. "ASEAN and the ZOPFAN Concept". Regional Strategic Studies Programme, Institute of Southeast Asian Studies Singapore, 1991.

Harpviken, Kristian Berg and Berg, Kristian. "Caught in the Middle? Regional Perspectives on Afghanistan". In: Kristian Berg Harpviken, ed. *Troubled Regions and Failing States: The Clustering and Contagion of Armed Conflicts*. Comparative Social Research, Volume 27. Bingley: Emerald Group Publishing Limited, 2010.

Harrison, S. Selig. "Dateline Afghanistan: Exit Through Finland?" *Foreign Policy* 41(41) (Winter 1980–1981): 163–187.

Hasan, Zubeida. "The Foreign Policy of Afghanistan". *Pakistan Horizon* 17(1) (First Quarter 1964): 48–57.

Hassan, Haniff Muhammad. "War, Peace or Neutrality: An Overview of Islamic Polity's Basis of Inter-State Relations". Rajaratnam School of International Studies (RSIS), 2007.

Hassman, Edith. "U.S. Foreign Policy: The Views from Vienna". *Executive Intelligence Review* 7(10) (March 1980): 55–57.

Haushofer, Karl. "Why Geopolitik?" In: Gerard Toal, Simon Dalby and Paul Routledge, eds. *The Geopolitics Reader*. London: Routledge, 1998.

"Hearings II: Committee on Government Operation, House of Representatives. United States Aid Operations in Laos: Seventh Report by the Committee. June 15, 1959. (86th Cong., 1st sess.)". Washington, DC: Government Printing Office, 1959.

Heiko, Borchert H. "Switzerland and Europe's Security Architecture: The Rocky Road from Isolation to Cooperation". In: E. Reither and H. Gärtner, eds. *Small States and Alliances*. Heidelberg: Physica-Verlag, 2001.

Herzig, Edmund. "Iran and Central Asia". In: Roy Allison and Lena Jonson, eds. *Central Asian Security. The New International Context*. Washington, DC: Brookings Institution, 2001.

Hwang, In K. *The Neutralized Unification of Korea in Perspective*. Cambridge, MA: Schenkman Pub. Co, 1980.

Inderfurth, Karl F. and Dobbins, J. "Ultimate Exit Strategy". *The New York Times*, 26 March 2009.

Jesse, Neal G. "Choosing to Go It Alone: Irish Neutrality in Theoretical and Comparative Perspective". *International Political Science Review* 27(1) (January 2006): 7–28.

Karsh, Efraim. "International Co-Operation and Neutrality". *Journal of Peace Research* 25(1) (March 1988): 57–67.

Khadduri, Majid. *War and Peace in the Law of Islam*. Clark, New Jersey: Lawbook Exchange, 2007.

Kittikhoun, Anoulak. "Small State, Big Revolution: Geography and the Revolution in Laos". *Theory and Society* 38(1) (January 2009): 25–55.

Kovac, Andras and Ruth, Wodak eds. *NATO, Neutrality and National Identity: The Case of Austria and Hungry*. Vienna: Böhlau Verlag Ges. m. b. H. & Co. Köln· Weimar, 2003.

Kunz, Josef L. "Austria's Permanent Neutrality, Reviewed Work". *The American Journal of International Law* 50(2) (April 1956): 418–425.

Langer, P.F. and Zasloff, J.J. "Revolution in Laos: The North Vietnamese and the Pathet Lao". RM-5935. RAND Corporation, September 1969.

Lawrence, J.T. *War and Neutrality in the Far East*. London: Macmillan, 1904.

Leonhard, Alan T. and Mercuro, Nicholas. *Neutrality: Changing Concepts and Practices*. New Orleans, LA: University Press of America, 1988.

Lyon, Peter. "Neutrality and Emergence of the Concept of Neutralism". *The Review of Politics* 22(2) (April 1960): 255–268.

Ma'aroof, Mohammad Khalid. *Afghanistan in World Politics: A Study in Afghan-US Relations*. New Delhi: Gian Publishing House, 1987.

Maass, Matthias. "The Elusive Definition of the Small State". *International Politics* 46(1) (2009): 65–83.

Machiavelli, Niccole. *The Prince*, Translated by W.K. Marriot. London: J.M. Dent, 1958.

Mackinder, Halford J. "The Geographical Pivot of History". *The Geographical Journal* 23(4) (1904): 421–437.

Maillart, Ella. "Afghanistan's Rebirth". *The Journal of the Royal Central Asian Society* 27(2) (April 1940): 224–228.

Martin, David, Hind, Philip, and Huges, Vernon. "Armed Neutrality for Australia". *Armed Neutrality Review* 1 (April 1988): 1–25.

McConnell, H. "The permanent neutrality of Austria: 1955–1962". (Masters Thesis, University of Ottawa, 1962).

McCracken, William D. *The Rise of the Swiss Republic: A History*. New York: H. Holt and Company, 1901.

Mueller, Wolfgang. "Peaceful Coexistence, Neutrality, and Bilateral Relations across the Iron Curtain: Introduction". In: Arnold Suppan and Wolfgang Mueller, eds. *Peaceful Coexistence or Iron Curtain Austria, Neutrality, and Eastern Europe in the Cold War and Detente, 1955–1989*. Vienna: LIT, 2009.

Nathan, Laurie. "Security Communities and the Problem of Domestic Instability". *Crisis States Program, Working Series Paper No.1*.

Neuhold, Hanspeter. "The Neutral States of Europe: Similarities and Difference". In: Nicholas Mercuro and Alan Leonhard, eds. *Neutrality: Changing Concepts and Practices*. New York, NY: University Press of America, 1988.

Oppenheim, L. *International Law. A Treatise*. London: Longmans, 1905.

Parker, James E. *Covert Ops: The CIA's Secret War in Laos*. New York, NY: St. Martin's Paperbacks, 1997.

Paul, Roland A. "Laos: Anatomy of an American Involvement". *Foreign Affairs* 49(3) (April 1971): 533–547.

Pazhwak, R.A. "Afghanistan's Policy of Non-Alignment". *Kabul Times*, 21 May 1962.

Rathkolb, Oliver. "Bruno Kreisky: Perspectives of Top Level US Foreign Policy Decision Makers, 1959–1983". *Contemporary Austrian Studies* 2 (1994): 130–151.

Rathkolb, Oliver. "The Foreign Relations between the US and Austria in the Late 1950s". *Contemporary Austrian Studies* 3 (1995): 24–38.

Rathkolb, Oliver. "International Perceptions of Austrian Neutrality Post 1945". *Neutrality in Austria: Contemporary Austria Studies* 9 (2001): 69–91.

Ratzel, Friedrich. "Studies in Political Areas: The Political Territory in Relation to Earth and Continent". *The American Journal of Sociology* 3(3) (November 1897): 297–313.

Reshtia, Sayed Q. *Khatirat-e Siyasi Sayed Qaseem Reshtia, 1311 to 1371. The Political Memoirs of Sayed Qaseem Reshtia, 1932–1992*. VA: American Speedy Press, 1997.

Reshtia, Sayed Q. *Afghanistan in 19th Century*. Kabul: Maiwand Publishing Co., 2010.

Roberts, J. Jeffery. *The Origins of Conflict in Afghanistan*. Westport, CT: Praeger, 2003.

Rolence, Jan Martine. "The Relevance of Neutrality in Contemporary International Relations". *Faculty of International Relations Working Papers*. University of Prague, 2008.

Ross, John F.L. *Neutrality and International Sanctions: Sweden, Switzerland, and Collective Security*. New York, NY: Praeger, 1989.

Roy, Oliver. "Has Islamism a Future in Afghanistan?" In: William Maley, ed. *Fundamentalism Reborn?: Afghanistan and the Taliban*, 199–209. New York, NY: New York University Press, 1998.

Rubin, Barnett. *The Search for Peace in Afghanistan: From Buffer State to Failed State*. Karachi: Oxford University Press, 2003.

Saikal, Amin. *Modern Afghanistan: A History of Struggle and Survival*. London: I. B. Tauris, 2006.

Schelbert, Leo. *Historical Dictionary of Switzerland*. Lanham, MD: Scarecrow Press, 2007.

Sekhri, Sofiane. "The Role Approach as a Theoretical Framework for the Analysis of Foreign Policy in Third World Countries". *African Journal of Political Science and International Relations* 3(10) (October 2009): 423–432.

Sherman, Gordon. "The Neutrality of Switzerland". *The American Journal of International Law* 12(2) (April 1918): 241–250.

Shinn, James and Dobbins, James. *Afghan Peace Talks: A Primer*. Santa Monica, CA: RAND Corporation, 2011. Accessed 21 October 2013.

Siegel, Charles. *Classical Liberalism*. Berkeley, CA: The Preservation Institute, 2011.

Singleton, Fred. "The Myth of 'Finlandisation'". *International Affairs* 57(2) (Spring 1981): 270–285.

Staten, Cliff. "U.S. Foreign Policy Since World War II: An Essay on Reality's Corrective Qualities". August 2005. Accessed 25 November 2013.

Steiger, Henry W. "The Swiss Army". *The Field Artillery Journal* 31(8) (1941): 575–578.

Stephen, Laurence and Erich, Margolis. "Concepts and Conceptual Analysis". *Philosophy and Phenomenological Research* 67(2) (September 2003): 253–282.

Stourzh, Gerard. "The Origins of Austrian Neutrality". In: Nicholas Mercuro and Alan Leonhard, eds. *Neutrality: Changing Concepts and Practices*. New Orleans, LA: University Press of America, 1988.

Stuart-Fox, Martine. *A History of Laos*. New York, NY: Cambridge University Press Cambridge, 1997.

Tadjbakhsh, Shahrbanou. "The Persian Gulf and Afghanistan: Iran and Saudi Arabia's Rivalry Projected". *PRIO Paper*. Oslo: PRIO, 2013.

The 1955 State Treaty and Austrian Neutrality, Available at: The Association for Diplomatic Studies and Training, Laos Country Readers. Interview with Samuel B. Thomsen, Political Officer at the US Embassy from 1967–1970, 10.

The Constitution of the Republic of Afghanistan, 1990. http://ezproxy.library. yorku.ca/login?url=https://www.heinonline.org/HOL/Page?handle=hein.cow/ zzaf0008&collection=cow.

"The Taliban: Engagement or Confrontation?" Hearing before the U.S. Senate Committee on Foreign Relations, 20 June 2000.

Thucydides. *The Peloponnesian War*. New York, NY: Random House, 1951.

Tomsen, Peter. "Chance for Peace in Afghanistan, the Taliban's Days Are Numbered". *Foreign Affairs* 79(1) (January–February 2000): 179–182.

Toye, Hugh. *Laos: Buffer State or Battleground*. London and New York, NY: Oxford University Press, 1968.

"Treaty Series No. 27 (1963), the Declaration and Protocol on the Neutrality of Laos, Geneva". London: HMSO, 23 July 1963.

Vaidik, V.P. "Afghan Non-Alignment: Changing Faces". *International Studies* 20(1–2) (1981): 239–255.

Viliam, Phraxayavong and University of Sydney. School of Geosciences. *History of Aid to Laos: Motivations and Impacts*. Chiang Mai, Thailand: Mekong Press, 2007.

Walt, Stephen M. *The Origins of Alliances*. Ithaca, NY: Cornell University Press, 1987.

Walt, Stephen M. "International Relations: One World, Many Theories". *Foreign Policy* 110 Special Edition: Frontiers of Knowledge (Spring 1998): 29–46.

Walther, Hofer. *Neutrality as the Principle of Swiss Foreign Policy*, Translated by Mary Hottinger. Switzerland: Spiegel Verlag, Zürich, 1957.

Waltz, Kenneth. *Theory of International Politics*. Boston, MA: Addison-Wesley, 1979.

Weitz, Richard. "Beijing Braces for Afghanistan 2014". *China U.S. Focus.* January 18, 2014.

Wengler, Wilhelm. "The Meaning of Neutrality in Peacetime". *McGill Law Journal* 10(4) (1964): 369–380.

Wicker, Cyrus French. *Neutralisation*. London: Oxford University Press, 1911.

Wright, Herbert. "The Legality of the Annexation of Austria by Germany". *The American Journal of International Law* 38(4) (October 1944): 621–635.

Zahra, Muhammcd Abu. "International Relation in Islam". In: *The First Conference of Academy of Islamic Research*, Cairo, 1968.

Zongyou, Wei. "In the Shadow of Hegemony: Strategic Choices". *The Chinese Journal of International Politics* 1(2) (2006): 195–229.

Zuḥaylī, Wahbah. *Athar al-Harb: fi al-Fiqh al-Islami* (In Arabic). Beirut: Dar Al-Fikr, 1998.

Zviagel'skia, Irina. "Russia and Central Asia: Problem of Security". In: Boris Z. Rumer, ed. *Central Asia at the End of the Transition*, 71–92. New York, NY: M.E. Sharpe Armonk, 2005.

Newspaper articles and online resources

"Afghanistan Dreams of a NATO-Free Future". *Russia Today*, 23 July 2010.

"Afghanistan's Region: 2014 & Beyond, Joint Declaration on Regional Peace and Stability". 17 November 2013. https://library.fes.de/pdf-files/iez/10307.pdf. Accessed 6 July 2020.

AP, "Britain Gets Private Word on Afghanistan". *Sarasota Herald Tribune*, 12.

"Article Three of the Constitution of the Islamic Republic of Afghanistan". Ratified on January 26, 2004. http://www.afghanembassy.com.pl/afg/images/pliki/TheConstitution.pdf. Accessed 6 July 2020.

"Carter Backs Afghan Neutrality". *Sarasota Herald Tribune*, 27 February 1980.

"Drastic Food Rationing in the Ruhr". *The Canberra Times*, 7 May 1947. Accessed 9 December 2014.

"Dulles Formulated and Conducted U.S. Foreign Policy for More Than Six Years". *The New York Times*, 25 May 1959.

"Fixing Failed States: From Theory to Practice". In: *Transcript of President Ghani's Lecture at Chatham House*. London, UK: The Royal Institute of International Affairs, 4 December 2014. https://president.gov.af/en/transcript-of-president-ghanis-lecture-at-chatham-house-the-royal-institute-of-international-affairs-fixing-failed-states-from-theory-to-practice/. Accessed 6 July 2020.

"Gilani for 'Neutrality' of Afghanistan in Future Initiative". *Indian Express*, 10 January 2010.

"Maddison Historical Data Covers Population by Country, GDP and GDP Per Capita Back to 1820". https://www.rug.nl/ggdc/historicaldevelopment/maddison /releases/maddison-project-database-2018?lang=en. Accessed 6 July 2020.

"Permanent Neutrality and Disarmament of Afghanistan". *Collection of Articles from a Seminar Held by the Academy of Science of Afghanistan.* Government Publication, 1989. http://catalog.acku.edu.af/cgi-bin/koha/opac-ISBDdetail.pl? biblionumber=26289. Accessed 6 July 2020.

"Report on Amir's Proclamation of Neutrality". Editorial of Siraj Al-Akhbar, 21 October 1914. Available Online. http://afghanistandl.nyu.edu/books/adl0616/ adl0616_v1_p03_000001.html. Accessed 6 July 2020.

The Moscow Conference 1943, "Joint Four Nations Declaration". https://avalon. law.yale.edu/wwii/moscow.asp. Accessed 20 September 2014.

"US and USSR Relations, Afghanistan Section, Available on the Website of the Association for Diplomatic Studies and Training (ADST)". https://adst.org/ wp-content/uploads/2012/09/US-AND-USSR-RELATIONS.pdf. Accessed 6 July 2020.

"USSR: Withdrawal from Afghanistan". *Director of Central Intelligence, Special National Intelligence Estimate*, 219, March 1988. https://nsarchive2.gwu.edu/ NSAEBB/NSAEBB57/us9.pdf. Accessed 6 July 2020.

Index

Note: Page numbers in **bold** indicate tables.

For Product Safety Concerns and Information please contact our EU
representative GPSR@taylorandfrancis.com
Taylor & Francis Verlag GmbH, Kaufingerstraße 24, 80331 München, Germany

www.ingramcontent.com/pod-product-compliance
Ingram Content Group UK Ltd.
Pitfield, Milton Keynes, MK11 3LW, UK
UKHW021423080625
459435UK00011B/132